KINGS CANYON COUNTRY

GUIDE TO KINGS CANYON NATIONAL PARK

BISHOP CREEK COUNTRY

SHAVER-DINKEY CREEK COUNTRY

KINGS CANYON COUNTRY

LEW AND GINNY CLARK

A Western Trails Publication

The twinkling stars of Sierra nights
Look down on the mountains wrapped in snow
A chorus of winds along the lofty heights
Mingles with the roar of streams below

Home of the rosy finch, polemonium, and cony
And alpine willow and cassiope dwell;
In meadows, chimneys, and landslides stony
The wildfolk of nature live in its spell.

Land of antiquity! Going back in time
For its glacial crags and cirques;
Engaging the elements of every clime
To carry on its tremendous works.

With summer's rain and winter's snow
The quarrying glaciers grind their flour;
And the rivulets and streams in canyons below
Carry the unending toil of creation's hour.

— LWC

ISBN 931532-20-5

Western Trails Publications
P.O. Box 1697
San Luis Obispo, Ca., 93406

LEGEND

Red on Maps

Main Trail with Pass

Other Trails

Cross-Country Trails

Park Boundary Line

Mileage Between Points 3.0

Bighorn Sheep Zoological Area

Wilderness Area

Black on Maps

Ranger Station

Campground

Main Road

Jeep and Four-wheel Drive Road

Corrals

Interpretive Programs

Lookout Tower

Marina

Picnic Area

Post Office

Telephone

Trailer Dump

Winter Sports

Topographical Map: ½" denotes 1 mile

Middle Fork of the Kings NPS Photo

TABLE OF CONTENTS

DIMENSIONS OF A WILDERNESS

Kings Canyon National Park not only is known for the giant sequoias of the Grant Grove paralleling the splendor of the magnificent stands of Sequoia National Park, but for the rugged, wild, spectacular high country of great granite crags, rushing torrents of crystal bright springs, and sublime flowered meadows.

The statistical dimensions of this vast wilderness are awesome. The deepest of all canyons in the Sierra are found in the basins of the Kings River and its two main tributaries – the South and Middle Forks. In the South Fork, at Cedar Grove (4635') the peaks of the Monarch Divide stand some 6400'-7000' above it with passes over the divide leading to Simpson Meadow more than 10,000' elevation. These passes require a steep climb of over 6000' out of Cedar Grove. In the Middle Fork of the Kings at Simpson Meadow (5910'), the surrounding peaks of the Monarch Divide south; the Cirque Crest (with Marion Peak, 12,719') to the east; and Tunemah Peak of the White Divide (11,894') to the northwest, create a canyon wall more than a mile high. At the junction of the Middle and the South Forks below Tehipite Valley the adjacent crest stands 7500' above the turbulent Kings. The maximum height at Spanish Mountain is 8200' above the water, which is deeper than the Snake River Canyon Walls or those of the Colorado River at Grand Canyon. The many deep canyons and rugged peaks surrounding them left by the glaciers are splendid in character, and, at places, chaotic to hike through.

The Kings Canyon Country was created by running water and flowing ice. In the Dinkey Creek and the North Fork of the Kings, glaciers formed a *mer de glace* of more than 1500 square miles in extent, as many confluent glaciers descended from surrounding mountain highlands. In the early ice ages, the longest trunk glacier flowed down the South Fork some forty-three miles. In the last ice age the Middle Fork glacier reached a length of twenty-eight miles.

Some sixty glaciers inhabit the deep, shaded fronts of towering crests with the largest abutting the Glacier Divide, the headwaters of upper Bishop Creek Basin, and the Palisades above Big Pine Creek. Their south and west basins contain more than a thousand lakes along the highest ramparts of the Sierra between the Glacier Divide above Evolution Valley and the Whitney-Muir crest below the Kings-Kern Divide. Glacial stairway lakes, such as Sixty Lakes Basin, cirque lakes as found in the Cartridge Lake Basin, and glacial polish on the canyon walls of The Citadel are all evidences of glacial forces that shaped this majestic, weather-mellowed land.

The geologic uplift of the great granite block of the Sierra Nevada accounts for the gradual rise to the crest on the western face and the sharp drop off the escarpment on the eastern slope. With the rugged terrain, high mountain canyons and jagged crests of the Kings Canyon National Park carved by the glacial action, any trans-Sierra highways are impactical. However, with the numerous east-west lateral trails, excellent backcountry mountain experiences are provided.

The many trails leading into the Kings Canyon Country spread out in an intersecting network from roadends, lakes, and resorts with pack stations in the west, north, east and south. The condition of the trails varies from year to year depending on the weather. The major trails are repaired and kept up regularly although some secondary ones are not always repaired from storm damages of a given season. Some years the budget for trail maintenance is smaller than needed to fully maintain a trail sufficiently. In the years of heavy snow during the winter, trails are opened late or sometines not at all, so it is important to check the condition of the trail you plan to use when you receive your Wilderness Permit.

The grandeur of this magnificent composite of tumbling waters, deep canyons, glacial barren cirques, rugged granite peaks, sky blue lakes, and flower-decked meadows is unique. Here in the Kings Canyon, you can find true wilderness that excels in quantity and quality.

Fork of the Kings
Wishon Reservo
HUME LAKE
Spanish Mountain
GNAT MDW.
Tehipite Dome
SOUTH FORK KINGS RIVER
MIDDLE FORK KINGS RIVER
MONARCH DIVIDE
KENNEDY PASS
GRANITE PASS
CEDAR GROVE
COPPER CREEK
SIMPSON MEADOW
Goddard Creek

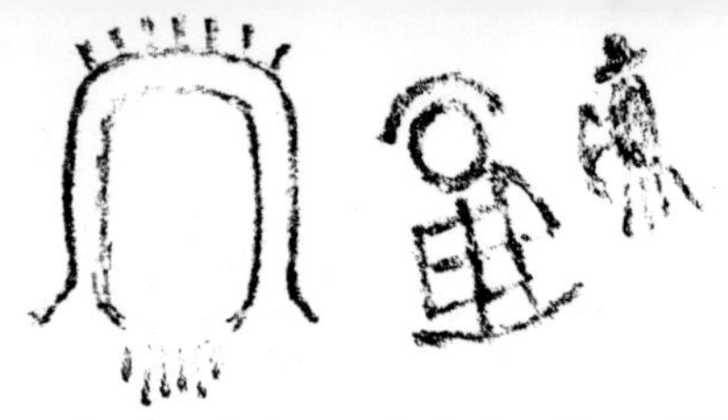

INDIANS

In the deep, secluded valley of Cedar Grove prehistoric Indians made this their summer base camp from which they travelled into the high country to hunt. They gathered the acorns and berries of the land and fished the streams and rivers. This remote valley with the protective granite walls of the South Fork of the Kings Canyon and the open, sunny floor made the Cedar Grove area an ideal home. The warm summer climate and nearly 5000' elevation was considerably cooler than the hot foothill country, as well as being closer to the source of food and trade routes.

Camps have been located in Cedar Grove, Simpson Meadow and up Bubbs Creek dating as far back as 1000 A.D. Many other sites have been found in the Kings Canyon area along streams and rivers. Some pictographs have been discovered near Tehipite Valley.

The Indians traded with the eastern Sierra Paiutes to whom they were closely related. Established trade routes were discovered through the Bubbs Creek and Woods Creek canyons, up to Kearsarge Pass. They exchanged their black oak acorns, berries, and buck skins for obsidian found in the volcanic regions of the Owens Valley and the nuts of the pinyon pines which were prevalent on the eastern Sierra slopes and high desert region. It is believed they also bartered for baskets, salt and rabbit skin blankets.

Other trails were found in the Kings Canyon National Park leading from Sequoia Lake, Grant Grove, and Sugarloaf Meadow to trans-Sierran trails via Cloud Canyon and Colby Pass, down the Kaweah River to Junction Meadow, up Tyndall Creek to Shepherd Pass.

All summer they gathered the food which was preserved for the winter months where they lived in the lower foothill regions out of the fierce mountain weather. Besides the berries and black oak acorns other sources of food were the yucca plant, manzanita and chia found in the drier lower slopes. They supplemented their diet with the abundant deer, bear, and rodents such as weasels, squirrels, and packrats as well as the bountiful fish found in the streams and rivers.

Many chipped stone tools, arrowheads, and soapstone cooking implements have been found. Although some fired clay vessels were uncovered in the archeological diggings, it is believed that baskets were used for the cooking of their food. The baskets were finely woven and fine enough for the cooking and holding of their mushy meal made from the ground black oak acorns. Fine grained stones such as granite were first heated in the fire, dipped in water to clear away any ash, and then carefully placed into the basket with the acorn meal and water. By stirring the mush and stones together, the food was cooked, well mixed, and the basket preserved from burning by the heat.

They were not a warlike people. Their relationship with the Owens Valley Indians became more like traders or cousins who look forward periodicaly to family reunions. There are numerous stories of their visits which lasted for a year or two on the other side of the mountain before returning home. Studies in langauge of the Owens Valley and the San Joaquin Valley peoples indicate a strong similarity in words describing such relationships. Also their need of one another in both economic and social affairs had developed this intertribal arrangement and consistent peaceful interchange.

The pictographs left on the granite boulders and cliffs in the Sierra are fading away. The moccasin tracks up the long valleys and over the rugged passes, though faint for a time, have beome the trails followed by the lovers of the high country.

HISTORY

Few white men travelled into the high country before 1860. With the warm climate of California foothills and forested mountainsides, along with the free pasture for grazing cattle and sheep, herding was profitable. The sheepherders were the initial substantial users of this region. But with their uncontrolled exploitation by the practice of burning of hillsides, damaging fragile mountain meadows, and over grazing the mountain slopes, public disdain and explorers and naturalists such as John Muir finally urged some forest protection.

The sound of sawmills began in the early 1860's as lumbermen cut down the giant sequoias and the pine and fir trees. From the Big Stump Basin many large trees were harvested by the Smith Comstock Company just for grape stakes and fence posts! With the advent of the flumes in the late 1880's the Converse Basin was stripped of some of the finest stand of sequoias.

In 1864, Professor Josiah Dwight Whitney led the first California State Geological Survey into the High Sierra, along with William E. Brewer, Charles F. Hoffman, Clarence King, James T. Gardiner and Richard Cotter. These early explorers and surveyors of the high country are remembered by the names of present peaks.

As the years passed many early mountain men ventured into this vast wilderness and viewed the rugged pinnacles, cirque basins, magnificent watersheds, frozen tarns, glaciers, and granite canyons. John Muir first explored the southern Sierra in 1873 having spent many years before in the Yosemite region. He travelled into the headwaters of the San Joaquin, Kings, and Kaweah rivers. In 1875 he explored the extensive sequoia groves found in Yosemite, Kings Canyon, and Sequoia National Parks. During 1875 and 1877 he penetrated the South and Middle Forks of the Kings River basins.

Prospectors travelled into the canyons searching for gold. One claim was near Kearsarge Pass but no great wealth was discovered. Hunting and fishing parties later journeyed into the high country as the region became publicized and known.

Sincere gratitude must be given to the park advocates, wilderness conservationists and special interest groups who fought so long in a bitter struggle to preserve the sublime beauty of the mighty Kings River. As one travels the highway along the river as it rushes through the rugged, rocky canyon to Cedar Grove, or hikes the trail up to the beautiful untouched Tehipite Valley, a deep appreciation should be felt for the protection of these canyons from exploitation for all times. The water and power irrigationists fought for many years in their strenuous efforts to dam the river and surrounding valleys, but finally compromised with the supporters of a power-free Kings River. The battles are not over as more power and more water is needed in our modern civilization, more and more dams are being considered in the foothills of the Sierra rivers today.

In 1940 the early battles and confrontations were cleared as President Franklin D. Roosevelt signed the bill to establish the Kings Canyon National Park. Prolonged discussions of the Tehipite Valley and the Cedar Grove area of the Kings Canyon were concluded in 1965 when they mercifully were added to the park. The Pine Flat Dam and other reservoirs such as Shaver and Huntington lakes were built to control the waters and usages of the Kings River as well as the other Sierra-based rivers flowing into the San Joaquin Valley.

GRANT GROVE VILLAGE

Azalea

The sylvan atmosphere among the beautiful giant sequoias is an ideal place to relax and escape the pressures of the urban life. The altitude of 6600' is higher and cooler than the floor of Cedar Grove. It is a safe family camping area among a woodland environment of azalea meadows, flowering shrubs, and wildlife association. Take time to explore this forest-land where Indians lived long ago and experience the wonders of this ecological community.

The National Park Service has an Information Center, conducts evening campfire programs and daily walks to interesting places, and maintains four lovely campgrounds for your pleasure. Some sites overlook the San Joaquin Valley to the west far below. An evening walk to Sunset Rock can highlight your visit. The daily Naturalist-conducted walks amid the giant sequoias and through mountain meadows are one-half day or less in time.

At Grant Grove Village is a post office, operating in the summer months, a chapel, gift shops, cocktail lounge, and accommodations at General Grant Lodge. The lodge is open from May to October, with cottages, sleeping and housekeeping type cabins. Check Government Service, Inc. Sequoia National Park, Ca., 93262 for reservations.

Wilsonia Lodge near the Grant Grove Village is a privately owned resort with hotel and cabin accommodations in a rustic atmosphere. There is also a restaurant, grill and fountain, and a modern grocery store. Reservations can be made at P.O. Box 808, Kings Canyon National Park, Ca.,93633.

Trails lead to Sunset Rock and campgrounds, General Grant Grove, Sequoia Lake Viewpoint and around meadows. The Park Ridge Trail offers panoramic views of the great Kings Canyon Country to the north and east. That trail proceeds up to the Park Ridge Fire Lookout.

General Grant Grove and North Grove can be reached by a surface road and has parking areas and picnic tables. At Big Stump Basin there is also picnic facilities. A day tour could be made down to Cedar Grove along the Kings River or to Hume Lake for swimming.

Other groves to visit are the Converse Basin Grove and the Boole Tree with its full-length scar. It was spared and left alone in the early lumbering days. Redwood Mountain Grove is one of the most beautiful, exemplifying a pure sequoia forest. Bearskin Grove can be reached by a surface road from Hume Lake along Tenmile Creek east around Lava Butte.

By taking the road to Horse Corral and continuing on the unsurfaced road northeast through the Sequoia National Forest, the great Kings River country can be viewed from Lookout Peak. Other jeep roads in the area were old logging roads when this land was stripped for lumber some years ago. Between Grant Grove Village and Lodgepole in Sequoia National Park are other groves and trails.

Eugene Rose

GENERAL GRANT TREE – THE NATION'S CHRISTMAS TREE

So much has been written about this magnificent sequoia that only a brief resumé is necessary. Discovered in 1862, it was named after Ulysses S. Grant, then President of the United States. It became more widely known in 1925 when it became the Nation's Christmas Tree. Here, on Christmas Day, at high noon, services are held at its base. Its age is estimated between 3,000 to 4,000 years old, with the greatest horizontal base diameter (40.3') of any known sequoia.

Height above mean base: 267.4'
Mean base diameter: 33.3'
Base circumference: 107.6'
Weight of trunk: 565 tons
Volume of trunk: 45,232 cu. ft.
Board feet content of trunk: 542,784 feet
Height to first large limb: 129.0'
Diameter of largest branch: 4/5'
Diameter 60' above ground: 18.8'
Diameter 120' above ground: 15.0'
Diameter 180' above ground: 12.9'

The base exceeds that of many city streets. At least 20 railroad cars would be required to move its main trunk.

A short, easy walk to the east on top of a huge, flat rock is an excellent vantage point to view and photograph the General Grant Tree. From here the great fire scar on the lower face of the tree can be seen.

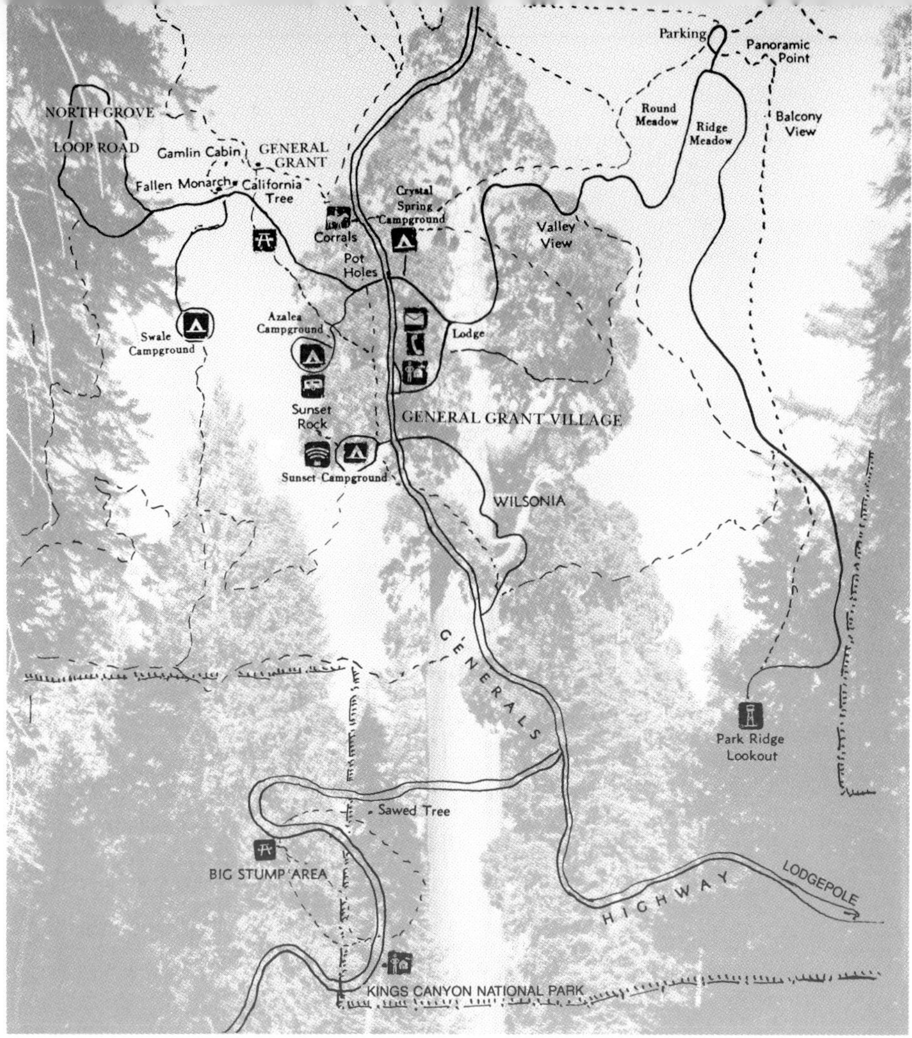

GENERAL GRANT GROVE

Indian "potholes" will be found at two places just after turning off the Generals Highway to the grove. These potholes were worn down into the rock by the Indians of long ago and were used as receptacles in which to grind their grain or acorns.

A few yards down the road is the Columbine Picnic Area with excellent facilities of tables and stoves in a setting of great trees contrasted with a flower-decked meadow. Those spending time at the Grant Grove will find this the best place to spread their picnic lunch.

Just before the Grant Tree parking area, to your left is the Martyr Tree, mute testimony to the efforts of a sequoia to overcome its wounds whether made by nature or man. There are two parking areas in the grove with no parking on the road. When taking pictures it is well to step off the road to prevent congestion of traffic.

Just left of the General Grant Parking Area, stands the TENNESSEE TREE whose bark at one time was practically all burned away. In the struggle for existence, this tree has extended its bark well within the hollow at the base. In one place a hole more than a foot wide and eight feet tall has been completely filled with this protective growth.

An exhibit case contains a summary contrasting the Coast Redwood (sequoia sempervirens) and the sequoias of the Sierra (sequoia gigantea).

GAMBLIN CABIN

In this lovely dogwood, cedar and sugar pine setting among the giants in 1872, Israel Gamblin and his brother Thomas, Vermont lumber people, came to settle. They homesteaded 160 acres within Grant Grove, filed a timber claim and built this cabin of "hewed log" construction. It was used as their home while they worked in the logging operation and grazed cattle in the Lake Sequoia region. When the General National Park was established, in 1890, the cabin was used as a storehouse by the U.S. Cavalry who patrolled the park until 1913. Later it became the quarters for the first park rangers stationed here. Just across from the doorway of this old cabin stands a huge sugar pine tree 22 feet in circumference.

CENTENNIAL STUMP

This great sequoia was cut in 1875 and a portion near the base was split into sections, hauled out to the San Joaquin Valley on ox wagons, shipped to Philadelphia where it was assembled and displayed at the Centennial Exposition the following year. It proved to be a failure as an exhibit because visitors seeing the lines which showed where the sections had been split for shipping, refused to accept it as a single tree.

CALIFORNIA AND OREGON TREES

These are about 270 feet high and have diameters of about 25 feet. They are considered the most beautiful of the giants in the southern Sierra range. (From here is an excellent view of the top of the Tennessee Tree.)

FALLEN MONARCH

Many years ago this tree was undermined and fell. The hollow log remaining is about 120 feet long, and can be transversed on the inside of the shell for its entire length. The large opening along the side near the base is more than 60 feet long, has an average width of almost 9 feet and a ceiling clearance of about 8 feet.

If it could speak, this old tree could tell many strange and wonderful tales such as how it gave shelter to Indians long ago, that it was a saloon in 1870, a dining room and kitchen serving early Park visitors and, when the Park was under the supervision of cavalry, it was used as a stable for some 32 head of horses. Campers and road workers used it as a shelter until recently, when Park authorities restricted all camping to designated areas away from the grove.

GENERAL LEE TREE

This sequoia, second in size to the General Grant Tree – the General Lee, has a diameter of almost 30 feet and is very symmetrical. It seems fitting that of the many great trees in this grove these two giants should symbolize our respect for two of our nation's outstanding men.

MATHER PLAQUE

In this quiet, unobstrusive setting the bronze plaque set into a large granite boulder is a fitting testimonial to one of the great workers in the program of the National Park Service – Stephen P. Mather.

FALLEN MICHIGAN TREE

Here might well be called the graveyard of fallen giants as great slabs and cross sections of trunks shattered when they fell. When standing, the Michigan tree was about 270 feet high and was known as the "Spring Tree." The spring which had once given moisture to the roots of this great tree eventually undermined it, causing it to settle off balance and fall. The spring still flows nearby.

NORTH GROVE

This special grove circled by a one-way road displays other fine specimens of giant sequoias that were once named after many of our soverign states. They have mastered storms of the ages, holding lofty heads high, being persistent in living despite fires and other destructive forces of nature.

THE BIG STUMP TRAIL

Just beyond the western entrance to Kings Canyopn National Park to the left is the Parking and Picnic area for the Big Stump Trail. The giant sequoia at the starting point of the trail, called the Resurrection Tree, was scarred by a lightning strike some years ago. Despite its cropped top, limbs grew to become a great tree. An excellent view of this tree can be had further down the trail, looking back at it.

This pristine forest now exhibits only sawdust piles an old rutted logging road, the old mill site and many stumps and debris. The Smith Comstock Company logged this once magnificent sequoia grove during the late 1800's. The Patee trees, the younger trees near the Burnt Monarch, were planted by a lumberjack in 1888 and have grown rapidly in the now protected surroundings.

Throughout this area shrubs and trees of the Transition Life Zone prevail. The sweet smelling mountain whitehorn, the beautiful Western azalea and the smooth reddish-brown-barked manzanita are the predominant shrubs. The ponderosa pine, the incense cedar, sugar pines with their graceful out-stretched limbs holding their large cones, and the white fir mature well in this environment. (See tree chart on page 56 for helpful identification.)

The BURNT MONARCH or "Old Adam" was one of the largest known giant sequoias before it was destroyed by fire many years ago. It is 97' in circumference and at least 2,375 years old. The Mark Twain Stump realistically demonstrates the size of a giant sequoia – the stump is 24 feet across. This tree was cut down for an American Museum of Natural History of New York exhibition in 1891.

Across the Park Highway, the SAWED TREE (.05 from parking lot) lives although its base was cut deeply some years ago but the tree resiliently survived.

NPS Photo

A special Christmas Service is held at the base of the General Grant tree as it is our nation's Christmas Tree. Other winter activities include sledding at Grant Grove, Lodgepole and Wolverton., Skiing at the Wolverton Ski Bowl offers a tow rope vertical rise of 80 feet for Beginners Hill; an Intermediate Hill of 800 feet long with a tow rope vertical rise of 150'; the Novice Hill of 1000 feet long with a tow rope vertical of 175'; and Baldy Hill, an expert run of 1000 feet long with a vertical rise of 320'. Group or private lessons are available as well as rentals for skis, poles, boots and rope tow grippers.

Wilsonia Lodge conducts guided hut tours which provide overnight use with space for families, friends or clubs. Skiing to the hut can vary from a 4.0 mile trip to more strenuous cross-country tours for the experienced that include panoramic vista views of the Great Western Divide under a snow mantle. The lodge provides accommodations, restaurant, store and ski rental.

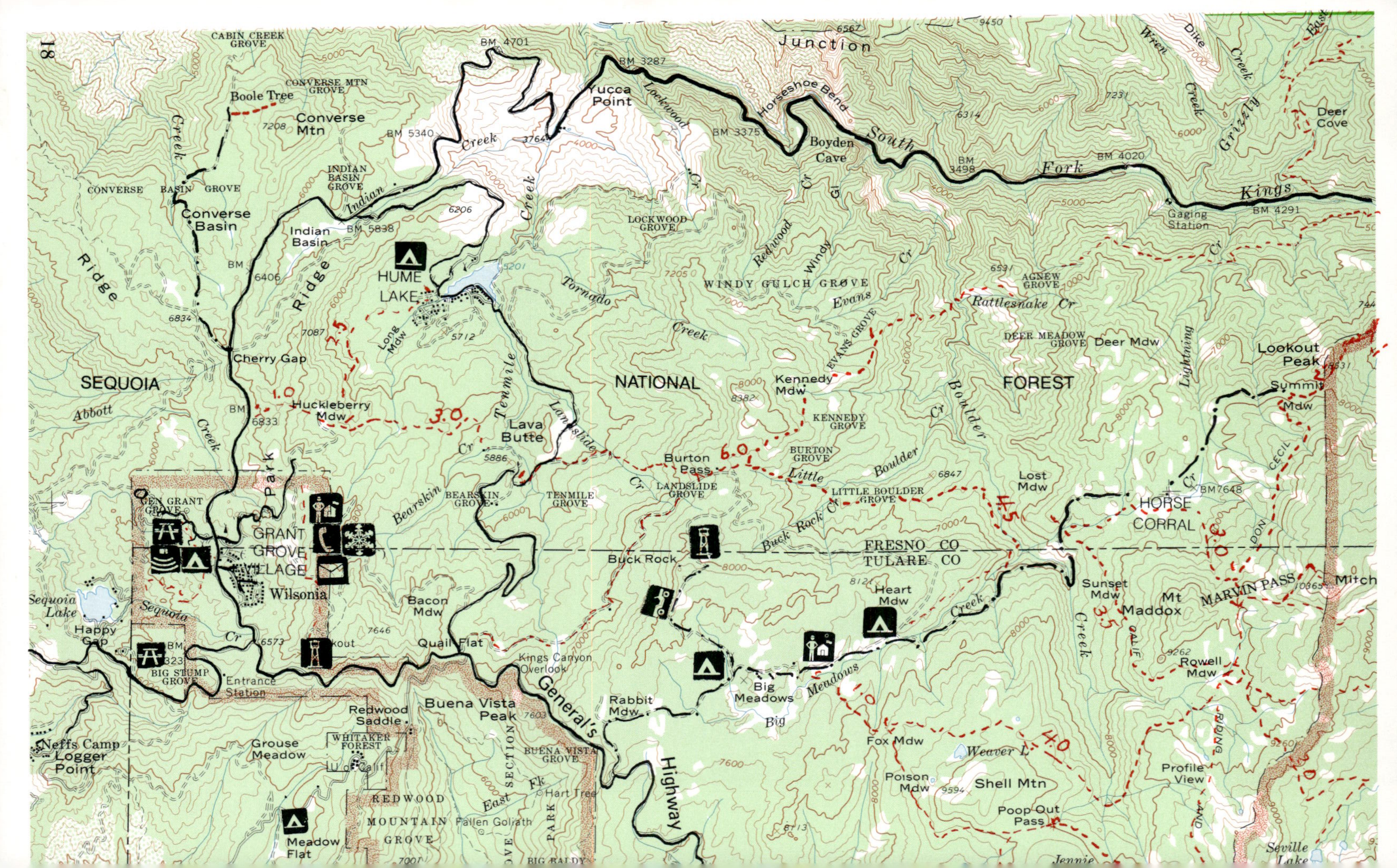
SEQUOIA
NATIONAL
FOREST
Junction
Horseshoe Bend
South Fork Kings
Boyden Cave
Yucca Point
Lockwood Cr
LOCKWOOD GROVE
Converse Mtn
CONVERSE MTN GROVE
Boole Tree
CABIN CREEK GROVE
CONVERSE BASIN GROVE
Converse Basin
Ridge
Abbott Creek
Cherry Gap
Indian Basin
INDIAN BASIN GROVE
Indian Creek
Ridge
HUME LAKE
Long Mdw
Tornado Creek
Tenmile Cr
Huckleberry Mdw
Lava Butte
Landslide Cr
LANDSLIDE GROVE
Bearskin
BEARSKIN GROVE
TENMILE GROVE
GEN GRANT GROVE
GRANT GROVE VILLAGE
Wilsonia
Park
Bacon Mdw
Quail Flat
Kings Canyon Overlook
General's Highway
Sequoia Lake
Happy Gap
BIG STUMP GROVE
Entrance Station
Neffs Camp
Logger Point
Grouse Meadow
Redwood Saddle
WHITAKER FOREST
REDWOOD MOUNTAIN GROVE
Buena Vista Peak
BUENA VISTA GROVE
Hart Tree
Fallen Goliath
Meadow Flat
East Fk
SECTION
PARK
BIG BALDY
Buck Rock
Burton Pass
BURTON GROVE
Little Boulder
LITTLE BOULDER GROVE
Buck Rock Cr
Kennedy Mdw
KENNEDY GROVE
WINDY GULCH GROVE
Windy
Redwood
Evans
EVANS GROVE
AGNEW GROVE
Rattlesnake Cr
DEER MEADOW GROVE
Deer Mdw
Boulder Cr
Lost Mdw
FRESNO CO
TULARE CO
Heart Mdw
Rabbit Mdw
Big Meadows
Big Meadows Creek
Fox Mdw
Weaver L
Poison Mdw
Shell Mtn
Poop Out Pass
Jennie
Sunset Mdw
Mt Maddox
MARVIN PASS
Rowell Mdw
Profile View
RIDING AND
Seville Lake
HORSE CORRAL
Lightning
Lookout Peak
Summit Mdw
CECIL
DON
Mitch
Gaging Station
Grizzly
Wren Creek
Dike Creek
Deer Cove
1.0
2.5
3.0
6.0
4.5
3.5
4.0
3.0

Frypan Meadow
East Fork
Comb Creek
FOREST
NATIONAL
PARK
NATIONAL
CANYON
SEQUOIA
KINGS
Lewis Creek
Hotel Creek
Pack Station
(one way)
North Mountain
Granite Creek
Mt. Hutchings
Lower Tent Meadow
North Dome
Copper Creek
Roads End
Zumwalt Meadow
Grand Sentinel
Avalanche Peak
Roaring River Falls
Roaring River
SOUTH FORK KINGS RIVER
Sentinel Dome
Cecil trail
Don Creek
Sheep Creek
Lookout Peak

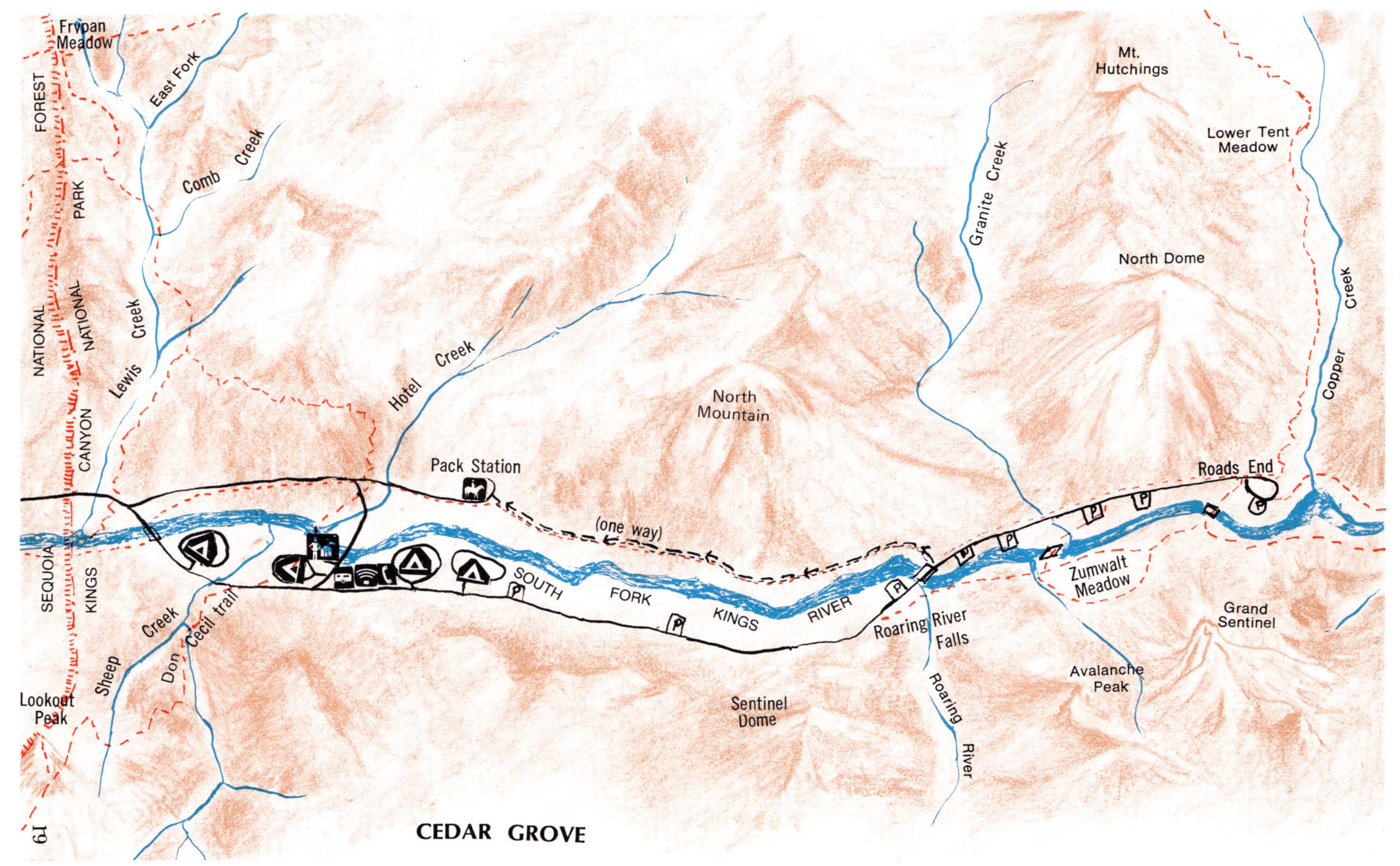

CEDAR GROVE

Road to Cedar Grove *Eugene Rose*

The twenty-eight mile road leading to Cedar Grove is both interesting and varied as it descends from the shade of the giant trees and flowered meadows, dips down with long switchbacks through old logging operations into the shadow of the deep cliff along the canyon walls of the turbulent Kings River.

Hume Lake, about three miles in from Highway 180 was man-made some fifty years ago for the lumbering business. Today there is a campground, store and a resort operated under the U.S. Forest Service. Swimming is one of its best attractions.

Boyden Cave is commercially operated, located near the junction of the South Fork of the Kings River and Windy Gulch, just east of Horseshoe Bend. It is a horizontal limestone cave, typical of the Sierra foothills with stalactitic draperies, cave pearls, and rimstone pools. The gentle graded trail through the cave leads to Upside Down City, Layer Cake, Drapery Room, and Christmas Tree.

CEDAR GROVE

Cedar Grove trailhead is the most popular entry into the headwaters of the South Fork of the Kings. Here, from more than a thousand square miles of granite-walled canyons flow the waters from the rugged slopes of the Great Western and Kings-Kern divides and from as far north as the headwaters of the South Fork of the Kings at Mather Pass.

Because of the valley's secluded position and difficulty of keeping the road open in the winter, extensive commercial developments have been discouraged. Basically, it is an area inviting a family camping vacation with warms days and cool nights in a wonderful mountain community with many miles of wilderness adventure possible.

This U-shaped valley of about a half mile wide and six miles long has four campgrounds beneath a forest of cedar and yellow pine with water and fireplaces. (No electrical or sewer connections.) There is an Information Center of the National Park Service; campfire programs; a pack station and corral; service station; a snack-bar as well as a market, and sleeping cabins without bath, heated by wood burning stoves (no advance reservations accepted). The lodging accommodations, service station and markets are open during June to Labor Day.

Scenic trails with magnificent vistas range from easy walks along the river to more strenuous hikes up the canyons. The Pack Station offers daily rides in the valley or extended pack trips into the backcountry. The Ranger-Naturalists conduct scheduled walks to various points of interest. Wildlife in the valley can be seen in their natural environment. Day trips can be made by driving back to Grant Grove Vilage, Converse Basin, Hume Lake or Boyden Cave.

MAJOR TRAILS LEADING OUT OF CEDAR GROVE

The trails are well maintained, and safe, varying from easy day walks to vigorous backcountry hikes. For extended overnight trips and backcountry travel, see the Cedar Grove Ranger Station for quota reservations and Wilderness Permits.

ZUMWALT MEADOWS

This scenic trail through open forest is good for beginners or for those who are acclimating for backcountry travel. The views of the tumbling river, tranquil flowered meadow, and majestic granite northern canyon wall makes this a memorable experience. The varying trees and shrubs, flowers and wildlife seen along the trail enhance this easy mountain walk.

RIVER TRAIL TO ROARING RIVER FALLS

An easy walk to one of the most beautiful attractions in Cedar Grove. These impressive falls can be reached by a short half-mile journey through shaded, open forest close to the river. Eastward the trail along the south side of the river leads to Zumwalt Meadows.

HOTEL CREEK TRAIL – LEWIS CREEK TRAIL CIRCLE TRIP

This trail starts easy, but beyond the Cascades it climbs steeply in a series of switchbacks before turning west, then through the open pine forest to the Lewis Creek Trail Junction. A good view is of the campgrounds, down the Kings River, Grand Sentinel, and Lookout Peak. It is about 5.5 miles to the Valley View. For the circle trip, take the Lewis Creek Trail down to the road.

LEWIS CREEK – FRYPAN MEADOW (5.3 miles)

The trailhead is two miles down the road west of the campgrounds and climbs up the old sheep trail through dry, hot, chapparral country, meeting the Hotel Creek Trail about 1.3 miles north. Carrying water is advisable. From that junction the trail follows up Lewis Creek through a pine forest to Comb Creek, then west to Lewis Creek, past the East Fork to Frypan Meadow. At nearly 8000', this meadow abounds with wildflowers during July and August. This all day trip has an ascend of over 3000'.

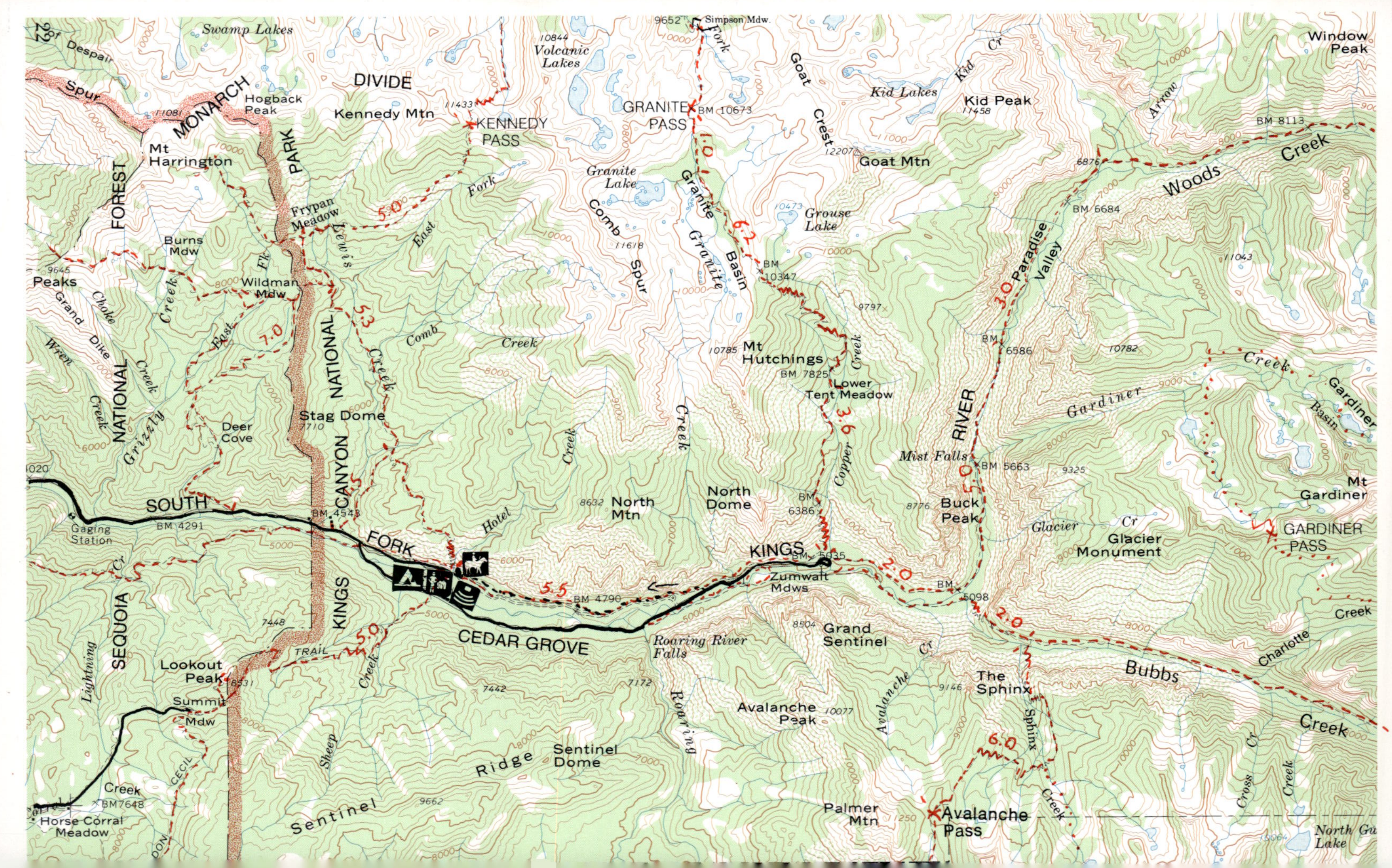
Swamp Lakes
Despair
Spur
MONARCH
DIVIDE
Hogback Peak
Mt Harrington
Kennedy Mtn
KENNEDY PASS
Volcanic Lakes
GRANITE PASS
Simpson Mdw.
Goat Crest
Kid Lakes
Kid Peak
Goat Mtn
Window Peak
FOREST
PARK
Frypan Meadow
Burns Mdw
Wildman Mdw
Peaks
Grand Dike
Choke
Wren Creek
Grizzly
NATIONAL
CANYON
Stag Dome
Deer Cove
Granite Lake
Comb Spur
Granite Basin
Grouse Lake
Mt Hutchings
Lower Tent Meadow
Copper Creek
Paradise Valley
Woods Creek
RIVER
Mist Falls
Buck Peak
Gardiner Creek
Gardiner Basin
Mt Gardiner
GARDINER PASS
Glacier Monument
North Mtn
North Dome
SOUTH
FORK
KINGS
Gaging Station
Zumwalt Mdws
Hotel Creek
CEDAR GROVE
Roaring River Falls
Grand Sentinel
Avalanche Peak
The Sphinx
Bubbs Creek
Charlotte Creek
Cross Cr
Avalanche Pass
Palmer Mtn
North Guard Lake
SEQUOIA
Lookout Peak
Summit Mdw
TRAIL
Sheep Creek
Sentinel Ridge
Sentinel Dome
Lightning
Horse Corral Meadow
CECIL

Mt Goddard
GODDARD
Muir Pass
Black Giant
Langille Peak
Le Conte Canyon
Dusty Creek
Martha Lake
IONIAN BASIN
Hester L
Little Jo Lake
Rainbow Lake
Charybdis
Mt Reinstein
Ambition L
Scylla
The Three Sirens
BLACK DIVIDE
Middle Fork Kings River
BLACKCAP BASIN
Mt McDuffie
Ladder L
Bighorn L
The Citadel
Division L
Ragged Spur
Disappearing
Enchanted
WHITE
Pearl L
Rambaud Creek
Wheel Mtn
Goddard
Rambaud Peak
Devils Crags
Cathedral Lake
Crown Basin
Finger Peak
Blue Canyon Peak
Gorge Creek
Mt Woodworth
Tunemah Lake
Great Cliffs
Ridge
DIVIDE
Creek
Tunemah Peak
Mtn Mdw
Blue Canyon
RIVER
Coyote Pass
Alpine
Windy Canyon
Kettle
Burnt Mtn
Bunchgrass Flat
Windy Peak
SIMPSON MEADOW
Rattlesnake
Creek
Dog Creek
Horseshoe Creek
Kettle Dome
Blue
Cr
KINGS
Dougherty Creek
FORK
Slide
Bluffs
Blue Canyon Falls
Lost Canyon
Creek
MIDDLE
East Fork
Tehipite Dome
Kennedy Creek
Ridge
Lake of the Fallen Moon
Tehipite Valley
Crystal Cr
Slide
Dead Pine
West Fork
Gorge of Despair
Slide Peak
Middle Fork
Glacier Lake
Swamp Lakes
Volcanic Lakes
Silver Spur
MONARCH
DIVIDE
Hogback Peak
KENNEDY PASS
GRANITE PASS
Creek

FRYPAN MEADOW TO SIMPSON MEADOW

From Frypan Meadow the trail turns to the East Fork of Lewis Creek, then north up the switchbacks to Kennedy Pass (10,800') on the great mountain range of the Monarch Divide which separates the South Fork and the Middle Fork of the Kings River. From the summit are fabulous views of the granite canyons below and the many majestic peaks and crests of the mountains beyond.

The trail descends west of Kennedy Creek and Dead Pine Ridge through beautiful country, then climbs up and over the wall onto the ridge at which point a more inspiring panorama is hard to contemplate: a breathtaking vista of the great country of the mighty Middle Fork of the Kings River. There is camping at Volcanic Lakes beneath the shadow of Comb Spur. The trail junctions with the Granite Creek Trail leading down to Simpson Meadow. Expansive views to the north include the Ragged Spur and the Goddard Canyon.

SIMPSON MEADOW

In this secluded valley, Simpson Meadow (5950'), surrounded by deep forest and granite walls, once made an ideal summer camp for early Indians. Potholes can be seen in the surrounding rocks. Sheepherders used this valley for grazing of sheep and cattle in the days before this region became a National Park. They came via the old Tunemah Trail from the west, that leads past Blue Canyon Creek, north of Burnt Mountain, above the rugged river canyon, past Bunchgrass Flat to Goddard Creek and Simpson Meadow, as shown by the cross country route on page 23.

In this remote, serene mountain meadow with lodgepoles and quaking aspens, campsites are available and fishing in the Middle Fork is rewarding, but rattlesnakes might be sleeping in the shade of the sagebrush.

The trip down the Middle Fork to see the beautiful granite Tehipite Dome standing more than 3500' above the valley floor is strenuous. The trail is long, sometimes rough along the the great stone south canyon wall of the Monarch Divide that rises 6000' above the river. The dome's unusual form with its sheer, smooth, symmetrical face is one of the most striking in the Sierra.

From Tehipite Valley at Simpson Meadow up the Middle Fork to meet the John Muir-Pacific Crest Trail, there is a continuous unbelievable high country experience as the trail follows along the roaring, tumbling waters in the shadow of overwhelming canyon walls, passing the narrow gorge and the spectacular Devil's Washbowl.

COPPER CREEK TRAIL TO SIMPSON MEADOW

For a day trip to Lower Tent Meadow (3.6 miles – 2800' climb).

Leaving the Roads End Trailhead at the Long Term Parking Area, the steep, strenuous ascend from the forested floor is a series of switchbacks through oak and manzanita leaving the glacially smooth Grand Sentinel, towering above Zumwalt Meadow, behind. Just east, past North Dome, the trail becomes more moderate in its climb. From here the unique twin glacial-eroded avalanche chutes of the Sphinx's northeastern face can be seen. This wilderness venture is enhanced with wildflowers along the trail and the tumbling, sparkling Copper Creek below. Campsites are available at Lower Tent Meadow where lovely Mt. Hutchings rises to its peak in the west.

Beyond Tent Meadow the switchbacks up to the awesome Granite Basin are steep. Marmots watch the traveler pass in this 10,000' alpine environment. Granite Pass divides the South Fork and the Middle Fork of the Kings River.

The trail to the State Lakes beneath the great Cirque Crest and Horseshoe Lakes nestled in the shadow of Windy Ridge starts north of the Lake of the Fallen Moon (BM 9609) going east. For continuation, see map page 29. There is excellent fishing and pleasant camping in a secluded wilderness, with high country vistas in an alpine solitude. This country is hard to surpass.

South Fork Near Zumwalt Meadows *Eugene Rose*

SOUTH FORK OF THE KINGS RIVER TRAIL

Mist Falls (4.0 miles; Paradise Valley (7.0 miles).

Leaving the Roads End Trailhead at the Short Term Parking Area, the trail ascends gently along the South Fork of the Kings River to Bubbs Creek. Although the first two miles are through the forested valley, the trail is hot and dry. At the Bubbs Creek bridge, the trail forks and the Mist Falls Trail climbs north following along the South Fork passing Buck Peak to the west and Glacier Creek to the east. Looking back, there is a fine view of the spectacular Sphinx to the south.

There are several beautiful cascades and waterfalls from both the Glacier and Gardiner Creeks entry into the South Fork. The best time to see Mist Falls is early in the season when the water of the river is high. Be careful when traversing the wet slippery surfaces! (Only very experienced cross-country hikers should attempt the rough, unpatrolled, old bushwacking, steep climb up the Gardiner Creek to the Basin. This is ROUGH country and has to be taken seriously.)

From Mist Falls the trail zig-zags up the river for three miles to lower Paradise Valley and through a forest cover it meanders three more miles further north to the Woods Creek Trail junction.

The trail up Woods Creek is a moderate-to-gentle climb with quaking aspens along the creek with a lodgepole forest cover to meet the John Muir-Pacific Crest Trail beneath the impressive Castle Domes.

HORSE CORRAL
MARVIN PASS
Mitchell Peak
Williams Mdw
Rowell Mdw
Comanche Mdw
Sugarloaf
Sugarloaf Valley
Roaring River
Palmer Mtn
Avalanche Pass
INDEFINITE
Cross Mtn
North Guard Lake
Sphinx
Sphinx Lakes
Moraine
Moraine Mdws
Moraine Ridge
Creek
North Guard
Crest
Mt Brewer
Ouzel
Country
Scaffold Meadows
Ellis Meadow
Ferguson
Brewer
Big Brewer Lake
South Guard L
South Guard
Longley Pass
Profile View
RIDING
AND
HIKING
TRAIL
Ball Dome
Seville Lake
East
Fork
West
Barton Peak
Scenic Mdw
Deadman
Barton
Cloud
Cunningham
Cr
Thunder Mtn
DIVIDE
JO Pass
Ranger Lakes
Kettle Peak
Lost L
Twin Peaks
South
Grave
Josephine Lake
Big Wet Meadow
Table Mtn
MILESTONE BASIN
Silliman
SILLIMAN PASS
Twin Lakes
Beville Lake
Ferguson Mdw
Table
Talus L
WESTERN
Midway Mtn
Cahoon Gap
Mt Silliman
Crescent L
Canyon
Glacier Ridge
Milestone Mtn
Kings Canyon National Park
Whaleback
Colby Lake
Kern Ridge
Clover
Silliman Mdw
Fableland
Big Bird Lake
Table Meadows
Colby Pass
Tokopah Valley
Tokopah Falls
River
Kaweah
LODGEPOLE
Aster L
Moose Lake
Pear Lake
Coppermine Pass
GREAT
Sequoia National Park
Heather L
Emerald L
Ski Hut
Elizabeth Pass
Mine
Glacier Lake
Gallats Lake
Kern - Kaweah

BUBBS CREEK TRAIL

After crossing the South Fork bridges and leaving Cedar Grove far behind, the Bubbs Creek Trail follows up the old Indian trade route to the east with a series of switchbacks meeting the Sphinx Creek Trail junction. Travelling under the forest of jeffrey pines, white fir, and lodgepole in this U-shaped canyon gorged by glaciers long ago with its crystal bright tumbling stream is a real high country experience.

Leaving the Bubbs Creek Trail with another series of bridge crossings, the Sphinx Creek Trail climbs moderately, sometimes rocky out of the lodgepole forest cover along the creek. A cross country, unmaintained trail can be made to Sphinx Lakes in the shadow of Mt. Brewer and the 'Sphinx Crest. Turning west and after the last creek crossing, there is a series of switchbacks up to Avalanche Pass (10,000') leading to Scaffold Meadows.

SHEEP CREEK / DON CECIL TRAIL

Named by early sheepherders, this trail starts at the Don Cecil trailhead near Campground 2 in Cedar Grove. Passing through this mid-mountain forest community of Mountain Misery, ponderosa pine, white fir and black oak, the climb is moderate. Look back to the great Monarch Divide to the north with peaks as high as 11,000', and enjoy the coolness of Sheep Creek and the small canyon before attempting the strenuous, hot and dry climb up to Lookout Peak (8531').

After crossing Sheep Creek the trail zig-zags and goes steep up to the Peak. There is an excellent view of the vast Kings River Canyon. At Summit Meadow wildflowers bloom throughout the summer. The Don Cecil Trail to Marvin Pass going south to J.O. Pass (9515') and Sequoia National Park traverses partly through the Sequoia National Forest which had in earlier years been logged and burned. The timber access road goes west to Horse Corral Creek and Meadow.

HORSE CORRAL TRAILHEAD

This is a good and easy entry into one of the most beautiful areas of the Sierra where camping is available and pleasant. The trail in this Sugarloaf Creek Country up to Scaffold Meadow passes through a forest cover and meadows with wildflowers. This comfortable subalpine mountain travel is a good introduction to more rugged high country beyond.

At Scaffold Meadow (7500') three trails lead to magnificent backcountry canyons. The Sphinx Creek Trail (2500' Ascent) with jeffrey pine, junipers, and red and white fir forest cover skirts around the east canyon wall of Moraine Ridge, ascending east of Palmer Mountain to Avalanche Pass (10,000'), then down the Sphinx Creek Trail to meet Bubbs Creek.

The Elizabeth Pass Trail (4000' Ascent) follows a steady climb up the beautiful Deadman Canyon through forest and meadows with a steep zig-zag near the final summit. A circle trip of real High Sierra adventure can be made by a cross-country access east over Coppermine Pass on Glacier Ridge, then down along Whaleback and Cloud Canyon returning to Scaffold Meadow. From Elizabeth Pass (11,200') the trail leads south to Bearpaw Meadow and the High Trail to Giant Forest or east to the Kern River and the John Muir-Pacific Crest Trail to Mt. Whitney.

The Colby Pass Trail (4600' Ascent) is a steady climb through mountain meadows and forest all the way to the sparkling Colby Lake where camping is available. From Colby Pass at the Great Western Divide, there is a fabulous panorama of Triple Divide Peak, the great Kern River Canyon country, the Kaweah Peaks Ridge and the vast high country of lakes and cirques of Sequoia National Park.

Both Elizabeth Pass and Colby Pass separate the Kings Canyon National Park and Sequoia National Park.

EASTERN APPROACHES

The most popular as well as easiest entry into the southern Kings Canyon Country is via the Kearsarge Pass. Be sure to acquire reservations for the Wilderness Permit early as quotas fill up fast. There are camping limitations as well as trail travel in this area. Perhaps plans could be made to enter this most beautiful country early or later in the season when it is somewhat less congested. When planning your trip, it would be wise to consider less concentrated, alternative routes and camping places. One of the reasons to venture into the backcountry is to "get away" from the tensions and stress of modern life and other people. The solitude necessary is best maintained by keeping away from over-populated paths. The secret of a good wilderness experience is to stay off the much traveled route except for short distances, then venture into the less publicized canyons. Every mile out you go, reduces people encounter and increases your enjoyment of the true High Sierra. By following the topo maps in this guide, you can find many marked trails to explore rugged glacial basins and a country rich in mountain splendor.

The Kearsarge Pass (11,823') entry provides the shortest route to the Rae Lakes-Sixty Lake Basin area. It is a moderate, four-mile climb from the Onion Valley road-end to the pass, then an easy descent to Bullfrog Lake to the junction with the John Muir-Pacific Crest Trail. There is no camping at Bullfrog Lake. Be sure to check the available overnight camping at Kearsarge Lakes. No wood fires are allowed – only chemical fuel stoves. There are some campsites at Charlotte Lake (1.0 mile west) on the Gardiner Basin Trail or in the large meadow down along the creek.

Fin Dome

North from the Bullfrog Lake and Charlotte Lake trail junctions on the John Muir-Pacific Crest Trail the switchbacks up to Glen Pass (11,980') are not as formidable as those on the Rae Lakes. The spur summit offers excellent views of the ragged Kings-Kern Divide to the south. This ridge separates the waters of Bubbs Creek and Woods Creek. The rocky, steep trail north down from Glen Pass typifies how rough some trails are.

What can surpass the view of Fin Dome reflected in Rae Lake. Or for one of the most memorable experiences of a Sierra night, to view Mt. Clarence King in the moonlight from one of the many beautiful blue lakes nestled in the granite of Sixty Lake Basin?

The remote sky blue lakes, sparkling streams and granite walls below Mt. Clarence King of Gardiner Basin can be reached by two unmaintained cross- country trails; west of Charlotte Lake over Gardiner Pass or west out of Sixty Lake Basin. Other less congested areas may be found up in the Baxter Lakes or Dragon Lakes basins or south in the Center Basin following the old John Muir Trail which went over Junction Pass.

Other entries to scenic and beautiful country are via the Baxter Pass (12,300') or Sawmill Pass (11,347'). However, these passes are not well developed or maintained, and both are long, arduous routes where special trail regulations apply through the narrow corridor of the mountain sheep reserve.

The California Bighorn Sheep Zoological Area includes the high eastern Sierra between Tunnabora Peak near Mt. Whitney to Mt. Perkins north of Sawmill Pass. Once very common in high mountains and desert plateaus of the west, the bighorn sheep are now quite rare. Depletion of herds was partly due to kills for meat by early settlers and miners. The largest factor, however, was the take-over by domestic flocks of sheep from Europe that introduced disease and over-grazed their food supply. Only small remnants of early herds are now found along the high east front of the Sierra. Fortunately, sheep's preference for alpine plants for food in the 11,000' to 14,000' elevations and their shy tendencies to seek privacy has somewhat stabilized their existence. Continual travel restrictions and people concern is needed in respecting the privacy of these high wilderness dwellers.

The trail from the roadend at the North Fork of Oak Creek ascending to Baxter Pass is a steep, dry climb but travelling through jeffrey pine groves and other shaded cover along the creek make this trail more pleasurable than the exposed steep, rough, long ascend up to Sawmill Pass. The forested bench at Summit Meadow has good camping. Once over the Baxter Pass there is camping in the sublime alpine Baxter Lakes basin. At the summit the spectacular panorama of colorful Mt. Baxter, to the north, Diamond Peak to the southwest, back down the North Fork of Oak Creek and the town of Independence to the east. Sawmill Pass Trail, now a cross-country route only, leads down into the remote Woods Lake Basin which provides excellent fishing.

To avoid traffic over Kearsarge Pass, another entry into the southern section of the South Fork of Kings Canyon can be made via Symnes Creek-Shepherd Pass (12,050'), down Tyndall Creek, up and over the formidable Foresters Pass (13,200'), down the John Muir-Pacific Crest Trail to Bubbs Creek. Another trip could be made from Shepherd Pass, down Tyndall Creek: go westward across the Lake South America-Milestone Basins, then north over Harrison or Lucy Foot passes down to lovely alpine Lake Reflection, or down East Creek to East Lake.

Up to Shepherd Pass it is a long, hot, rough trail similar to those of all eastern Sierra entries into the Kings Canyon Country. It follows through a deserty area at the lower elevations then climbs steeply to a ridge between Symnes and Shepherd Creeks. Water is scarce until reaching the upper level. Anvil Camp (10,000') is a good place for an overnight stop. Once over the crest it is downhill all the way along Tyndall Creek into the Upper Kern.

Castle Domes
Woods
Creek
KINGS
King Spur
Mt Clarence King
Gardiner Basin
Mt Gardiner
GARDINER PASS
Mt Cotter
Sixty Lake Basin
South Fork
JOHN MUIR
Stocking Lake
Mt Baxter
Baxter Lakes
BAXTER PASS
Summit Mdw
JOHN
North
California
Indian Rock
Black Canyon
Thibaut
Diamond Peak
Bighorn Sheep
Mt Mary Austin
Charlie Canyon
Little Onion Valley
South
Fin Dome
Rae Lakes
Dragon Lake
Parker Lakes
Sardine Lake
Tub Springs
MUIR
CANYON
GLEN PASS
Painted Lady
Dragon Peak
Kearsarge Peak
INDEPENDENCE
Charlotte Creek
Mt. Rixford
Mt Gould
Charlotte L
Bullfrog Lake
KEARSARGE PASS
Big Pothole Lake
Pack Station
ONION VALLEY
Lime Canyon
Mt Bago
Bubbs Creek
NATIONAL
Kearsarge Pinnacles
Vidette Meadow
Independence Peak
INYO CO
WILDERNESS
Pinyon
Junction Mdw
Creek
BOUNDARY
PACIFIC
FRESNO CO
TULARE CO
University Peak
North Guard Lake
East Vidette
West Vidette
West Spur
Vidette
East Spur
Center Basin Crags
Center Basin
Mt Bradley
Guard
East
East L
Golden Bear Lake
Zoological
North Guard
Ouzel Creek
The Minster
PARK
Center Peak
Symmes Creek
Mt. Brewer
Deerhorn Mtn
CREST
Mt Stanford
Ericsson Crags
Lake Reflection
HARRISON PASS
DIVIDE
Mt Keith
South Guard
Lucys Foot Pass
Mt Ericsson
FORESTER PASS
Junction Peak
Anvil Campground
INDEPENDENCE
Longley Pass
Mt Jordan
KERN
Mt Genevra
Caltech Peak
Lake South America
Williamson
KINGS
Thunder Mtn
SEQUOIA
NATIONAL
Diamond Mesa
PARK
SHEPHERD PASS
Area
TRAIL
Table Mtn
MILESTONE
BASIN
Tyndall Creek
Mt Tyndall
Mt. Williamson
Midway Mtn
Wright Lakes
Mt Versteeg
Lake Helen of Troy
Trojan Peak
4.0
2.0
4.0
1.5
2.5
8.5
3.0
3.0
4.0
6.0
6.0
2.0

BISHOP PASS
Temple Crag
Contact Pass
Mt Winchell
Dusy Basin
Palisade Glacier
Mt Sill
Elinore Lake
Kid Mtn
North Palisade
Columbine Peak
Barrett Lakes
Knapsack Pass
Giraud Peak
Palisade Basin
Palisade Crest
Finger L
JOHN
Middle Palisade Glacier
Middle Palisade
Disappointment Peak
Southfork Pass
The Thumb
Birch Lake
Birch Mtn
MUIR
GROUSE MDWS
Deer Mdw
Glacier Cr
TRAIL
Palisade Lakes
JOHN MUIR
Palisade Creek
Cataract Cr
Mt Bolton Brown
Mt Prater
WILDERNESS
Mt Shakspere
MATHER PASS
Amphitheater Lake
Observation Peak
Split Mtn
Red Lake
Devils Washbowl
Upper Basin
INYO CO
FRESNO CO
Windy Cliff
Dumbbell Lakes
Cardinal Lake
Cardinal Mtn
Vennacher Needle
MUIR - PCT
Taboose Pass
Lake Basin
Triple Falls
Cartridge Creek
CARTRIDGE PASS
Mt Ruskin
Marion Lake
Red Point
Striped Mtn
Windy Ridge
South Fork
Marion Peak
CREST
RIVER
Bench Lake
Horseshoe Lakes
Lake Marjorie
Mt Pinchot
Mt Wynne
PINCHOT PASS
State Peak
Mt Ickes
State Lakes
KINGS
Arrow Peak
Crater Mtn
Dougherty Peak
Blanco
Arrow Ridge
CIRQUE
White Fork
TRAIL
N Fk
Pyramid Peak
BM 10346
FORK
Muro
Creek
Window Peak
Kid Cr
SOUTH
Castle Domes
Woods Creek
Kid Lakes
Kid Peak
Arrow
BM 8113
BM 8492

Beautiful Bench Lake *Eugene Rose*

The Taboose Pass (11,360') entry into the upper basin of the South Fork of the Kings is for stalwart hikers as the route is long, hot, and a dry climb up to the summit. The view, once there, however, is rewarding – to the east across Owens Valley is the White-Inyo Mountains, and extensive panorama westward looking down into the main canyon of the South Fork, and Mt. Ruskin and Striped Mountain to the south.

Once over the Pinchot Pass (12,100') one of the most beautiful, the John Muir-Pacific Crest Trail enters the upper basin of the South Fork with the many lakes, streams, and lateral moraines below Mather Pass (12,080'). The John Muir-Pacific Crest Trail is well maintained, passes through high, open benches and across wide flower-decked meadows, down deep canyons where the rushing streams drown out all sounds. The trail follows along Lake Marjorie under the rocky cliffs of Mt. Ickes and goes over two of the loveliest passes in the Sierra – Mather and Pinchot.

A trip into the Cartridge Creek and Lake Basin amid an alpine environment of tundra meadows and granite offers a less populated area for camping in a fragile land. Beyond the first steep switchbacks from the South Fork north, the trail follows a less strenuous climb to Cartridge Pass (11,750'). The former route into the Lake Basin was up Cartridge Creek from the Middle Fork of the Kings and was the route of the John Muir Trail before the Mather Pass was completed. The Cartridge Creek Trail is now unmaintained, very rough and difficult to travel.

From Mather Pass to Grouse Meadow the trail descends 3750' first down the rocky talus past the sublime Palisades Lakes, then down the deep gorge known as the Golden Stairway, and finally along Palisades Creek to meet the Middle Fork of the Kings River and the lovely Grouse Meadow. From Deer Meadow it is possible to climb the steep grade up Cataract Creek on an unmaintained trail to Amphitheater Lake that has reportedly good fishing.

BIG PINE COUNTRY

The outstanding feature of Big Pine Creek is the Palisade Glacier, the largest in the Sierra with an area covering some three-fourths of a square mile. The Middle Palisade Glacier at the head of the South Fork of Big Pine Creek is smaller but just as jagged and impressive. Typical of the Sierra glaciers, they lie close up against the shaded north wall of the 14,000' Palisade Crest and are the most southerly glaciers in the United States. At one time, during the Ice Age, the glaciers extended down Big Pine Creek to First Bridge Campground (5100'). The glaciers are still active, moving in one season perhaps as much as forty feet. The milky green waters of the lakes below the glaciers are evidence of their action, grinding granite boulders into fine glacial flour. In these basins lie magnificent, gentle wilderness in all its natural beauty.

Plan at least two days to make a round trip to visit the Palisade Glacier. Climbing the glacier requires special equipment and skills and should be attempted only by experienced climbers. Wilderness Permits are required for all trips, even for one day duration as it is in the John Muir Wilderness.

The fishing both in stream and lake in the Big Pine Lakes basin and up the South Fork is extremely good for eastern brook, rainbow trout and some golden. There are U.S. Forest Service campgrounds and backcountry parking at the roadend. The glacier pack train offers one day to extended trips into the backcountry or to visit Palisade Glacier. Glacier Lodge in a beautiful, peaceful mountain setting, has accommodations, a general store and restaurant.

There are no trails or mountain passes leading from Big Pine Creek into the Kings Canyon National Park. The only trail to the John Muir-Pacific Crest Trail is by way of Bishop Creek. The trail follows around Baker Lake, goes over the ridge to Green Lake and down to South Lake.

There are seven main lakes in the Big Pine Lake basin, with First Lake being only 3.0 miles from roadend with a moderate climb. It is about 7.5 miles from the roadend to Palisade Glacier with very strenuous hiking, especially beyond the lake basin.

Palisade Glacier *Rocky Rockwell*

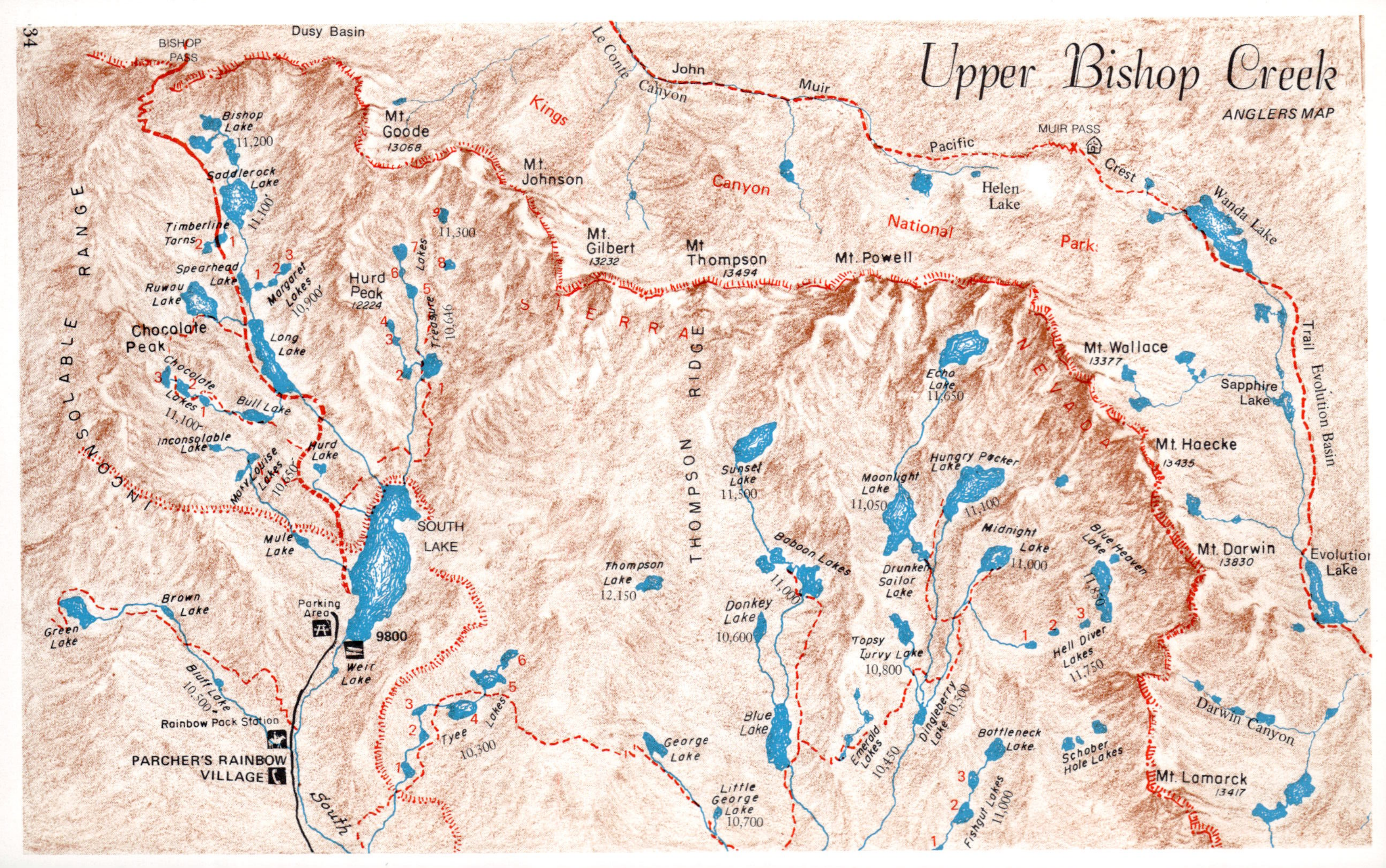

Upper Bishop Creek
ANGLERS MAP
BISHOP PASS
Dusy Basin
Le Conte
John
Canyon
Muir
Kings
Canyon
Pacific
MUIR PASS
Crest
National
Park
Helen Lake
Wanda Lake
Trail
Evolution Basin
Evolution Lake
Sapphire Lake
Mt. Wallace 13377
Mt. Haecke 13435
Mt. Darwin 13830
Darwin Canyon
Mt. Lamarck 13417
Mt. Goode 13068
Mt. Johnson
Mt. Gilbert 13232
Mt Thompson 13494
Mt. Powell
SIERRA NEVADA
THOMPSON RIDGE
INCONSOLABLE RANGE
Bishop Lake 11,200
Saddlerock Lake 11,100'
Timberline Tarns
Spearhead Lake
Margaret Lakes 10,900'
Ruwau Lake
Chocolate Peak
Long Lake
Chocolate Lakes 11,100'
Bull Lake
Inconsolable Lake
Mary Louise Lakes 10,650'
Hurd Lake
Hurd Peak 12224
Treasure Lakes 10,646
11,300
SOUTH LAKE
9800
Mule Lake
Parking Area
Weir Lake
Brown Lake
Green Lake
Bluff Lake 10,500'
Rainbow Pack Station
PARCHER'S RAINBOW VILLAGE
South
Tyee Lakes 10,300
Thompson Lake 12,150
George Lake
Little George Lake 10,700
Sunset Lake 11,500
Baboon Lakes 11,000
Donkey Lake 10,600
Blue Lake
Echo Lake 11,650
Moonlight Lake 11,050
Hungry Packer Lake 11,100
Drunken Sailor Lake
Topsy Turvy Lake 10,800
Emerald Lakes 10,450
Dingleberry Lake 10,500
Midnight Lake 11,000
Blue Heaven Lake 11,850
Hell Diver Lakes 11,750
Bottleneck Lake
Schober Hole Lakes
Fishgut Lakes 11,000

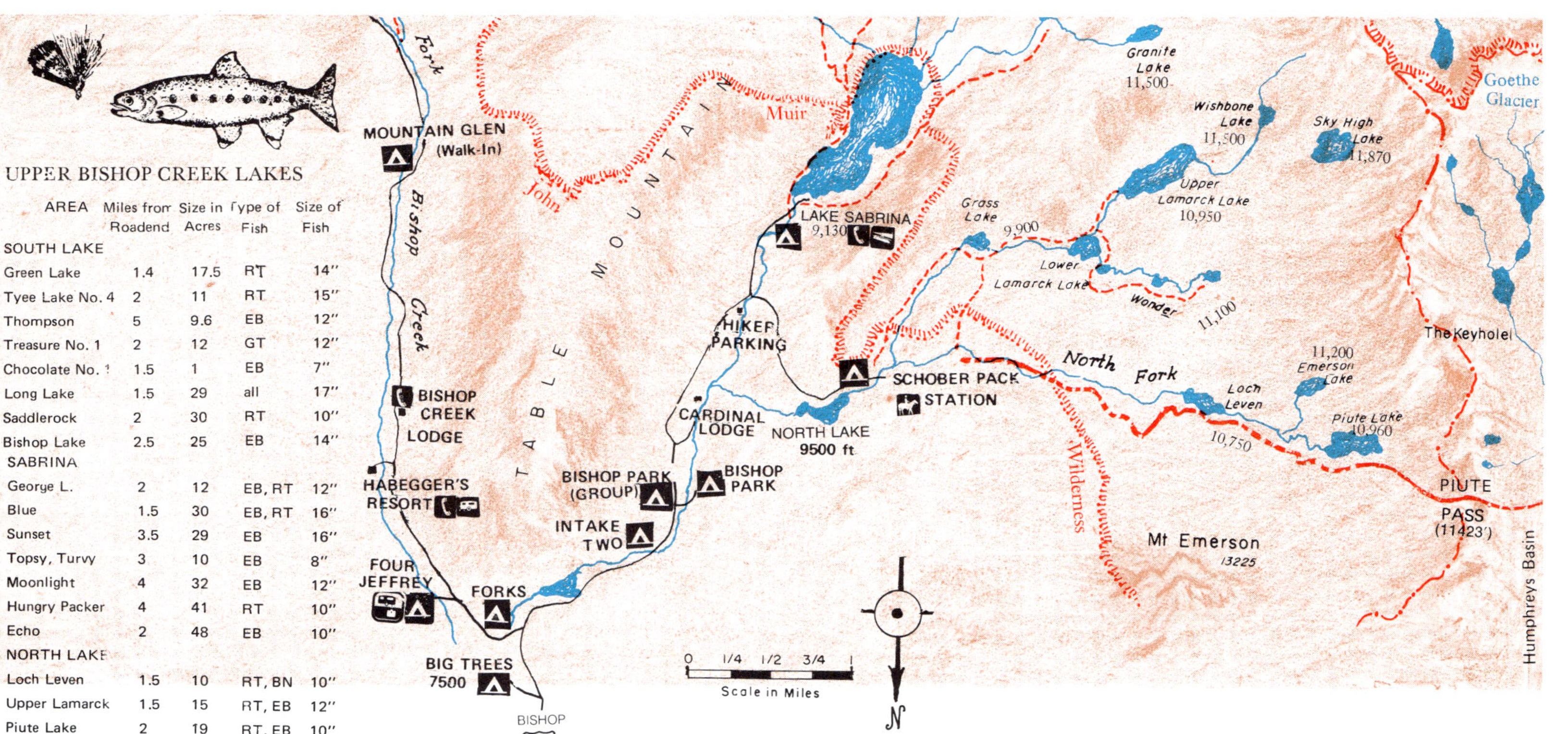

UPPER BISHOP CREEK LAKES

AREA	Miles from Roadend	Size in Acres	Type of Fish	Size of Fish
SOUTH LAKE				
Green Lake	1.4	17.5	RT	14"
Tyee Lake No. 4	2	11	RT	15"
Thompson	5	9.6	EB	12"
Treasure No. 1	2	12	GT	12"
Chocolate No. 1	1.5	1	EB	7"
Long Lake	1.5	29	all	17"
Saddlerock	2	30	RT	10"
Bishop Lake	2.5	25	EB	14"
SABRINA				
George L.	2	12	EB, RT	12"
Blue	1.5	30	EB, RT	16"
Sunset	3.5	29	EB	16"
Topsy, Turvy	3	10	EB	8"
Moonlight	4	32	EB	12"
Hungry Packer	4	41	RT	10"
Echo	2	48	EB	10"
NORTH LAKE				
Loch Leven	1.5	10	RT, BN	10"
Upper Lamarck	1.5	15	RT, EB	12"
Piute Lake	2	19	RT, EB	10"

Five varieties of trout are found in the 83 lakes in the upper Bishop Creek area: Eastern Book – 58; Rainbow – 36; Golden – 9; Brown – 5; and Kamloops Rainbow – 3. Nearly all of the lakes are less than three hours one way from road ends at South Lake, Lake Sabrina and North Lake. With the exception of these lakes, all are above 10,000′ in elevation – 40 are above 11,000′ and Thompson Lake is 12,150′. Hiking at these elevations require your serious concern about your general physical condition – pace yourself accordingly.

South Lake Panorama L. Dean Clark

BISHOP CREEK COUNTRY

This wonderful vacation land in the great High Sierra also is one of the most accessible into the Middle Fork of the Kings Canyon region.

Pauite Indians of long ago first inhabited this beautiful region of the Owens Valley. They made their camps along the streams flowing from the Sierra canyons. Piute Creek and Pass were named after these early people with a spelling variation of their name. The first white man entered this region in 1833, but it wasn't until 1861 that Samuel A. Bishop with his wife, a few followers and six hundred head of cattle first settled this area. From then on, other settlers came, prospectors and miners, farmers and by the early 1900's all the land was homesteaded. It was not always a peaceful settlement, as there were wars with the Pauites.

In the early 1900's Mr. Gaylord Wilshire founded the Wilshire-Bishop Mine which produced gold on a large scale. The ore was mined by a 600' shaft; the first 100 feet was vertical with the remaining 500 feet inclined. The ore carried $10 to $12 per ton which was approximately 99% gold, with a little copper and silver. The ore-body occurred along a zone of fracturing in the central portion of a body of quartize which was partially enclosed by intrusive granite and monzonite. Later in 1933 this mine was taken over by the Cardinal Gold Mining Company which consisted of 34 claims, twelve of which were patented. In November of 1937 the production was up to $1,570,000. In the next year operations ceased and the weather and time since then has erased all the major buildings and only old foundations can be seen of the original structures. There is gold as well as tungsten in the mine but there is no operation today. There were other mines along Bishop Creek, the Moffatt Mine just below the junction to South Lake, but the principle source of gold was the Wilshire-Bishop Creek Mine.

The Indians and miners are legends and history but the cattlemen still graze their herds. Each year in the town of Bishop they celebrate their annual Mule Days and during the summer hold rodeos. It is a vacation land with true western flavor, a paradise for fishermen, hunters, campers, climbers, hikers, and nature lovers. Bishop Creek country is rich in history, beauty and recreational opportunities, as well as being the most accessible passageway to the great Middle Fork of the Kings River country.

The Bishop Pass (11,972') is lower than other Eastern entries into the Middle Fork of the Kings River. Above South Lake the trail follows the beautiful valley enclosed by the west with the Thompson Ridge and on the east by Inconsolable Range. The main trail follows along a dozen lakes, each with excellent fishing. There is an extensive trail system within this great basin to the various lakes and all are well maintained and well marked.

In the Bishop Creek Basin one-day fishermen or overnight hikers have a lot to choose from in the many lakes and streams of three great basins – the South Fork, Middle Fork and North Fork of Bishop Creek. Fish are planted by the California Fish and Game into some eighty-three lakes and many miles of streams. Camping facilities maintained by the U.S. Forest Service vary from campsites with dumping stations for trailers and motor homes, rustic campsites along streams, and walk-in camps for hikers or those who enjoy walking away from the road and being in a natural mountain environment.

There are three lodges below South Lake with cabin accommodations, restaurants, cafes, trailer park, stores with fishing and limited food supplies, and a pack station.

At Parchers Rainbow Village is public telephone, cafe, store with sundries and fishing supplies, cabins, boat rental, showers and firewood. The Rainbow Pack Station is located here.

Haebeggers offers a cafe, gift shop, fishing supplies, laundry, public telephone, showers, firewood, propane, trailer park and trailer rentals.

Bishop Creek Lodge sells gasoline, groceries and sundries, fishing supplies, firewood and propane. They also have a public telephone, a restaurant, room and cabin rentals and showers.

At Lake Sabrina on the Middle Fork of Bishop Creek is a cafe, gasoline for boats, with sundries and fishing supplies, and boat rentals and a public telephone.

Cardinal Village is a great place to enjoy the beauties of Bishop Creek Country while fishing and relaxing. There are cabins, a store, and a lodge where cocktails and meals are served. Some of the old cabins from the Cardinal Mining days are used for lodgings. The cabin called "Drunken Sailor" was once the old schoolhouse up at the mine.

At North Lake Schober's Pack Station has pack trips going into the good fishing areas of Bishop Creek, Humphrey's Basin or French Canyon as well as deer hunting trips in the fall.

Evolution Crest-Sabrina Basin

Rocky Rockwell

There are three pack stations that offer daily rides, saddle parties and extended pack trips into the backcountry of the Kings River Country: Rainbow Pack outfit at South Lake near Parchers Camp, Schober Pack Station located in the North Lake basin, and Pine Creek Saddle and Pack Station north of Bishop that enters Humphrey's Basin and French Canyon. There are many types of trips to select from these corrals. Some packers are available for hunting parties in the fall.

DAY TRIP: Hire a horse, leave early and return horse before dark. Guides may be hired for one day.

SPOT TRIP: They will take you to a campsite of your choice in the backcountry, leave you there for a specified period of time and return to take you out. Cost is determined by the distance packed in and the number of stock needed for your gear and food.

EXTENDED TRIP: The packer and stock will remain with the party, staying at one camp and making side trips for fishing or travel along the trails. The party furnishes all food and camping gear.

ALL EXPENSE TRIP: Packers supply the guide, stock, food, equipment except for sleeping and personal gear.

CACHES may be packed in and left in a designated stop in the backcountry for group or extended travel along the trail.

When consulting the pack stations for reservations and type of trip you plan, they can suggest various interesting trips. One possible loop trip is via Bishop Pass, down Dusy Basin, along the John Muir-Pacific Crest Trail, over Muir Pass, down Evolution Valley, up Piute Canyon, over Piute Pass into the Bishop Creek basin.

Muir Pass Hut

JOHN MUIR-PACIFIC CREST TRAIL (viewed from Kings River Country)

To better visualize the great Sierra Nevada Crest from the Kings River Country the pictorial profile illustrates entries and passes along the John Muir-Pacific Crest Trail.

With most of this region above timberline, the rock formations are so exposed that geologists can study and determine the glacial history and development of the Sierra block. However, these ragged peaks, steep chutes and loose talus slopes all encourage the mountaineer to seek out and explore the wonders of this land. There are peaks to scale for all degrees of ability and experience from cross-country travel to technical rock climbers. A good guide to consult is *Mountaineers Guide To The High Sierra* put out by the Sierra Club.

Although the main trunk streams and rivers of the Sierra flow through the San Joaquin Valley eventually into the Pacific Ocean, their many tributary headwaters lie close to the main Sierra crest in a generalized north-south pattern. Ancient glaciers moved down these valleys and carved out deep U-shaped canyons with resulting east-west headwalls. Those found along the John Muir-Pacific Crest Trail in the Kings River country are:

LeConte Canyon and Evolution Basin (Muir Pass, 11,955')
Upper Basin and Palisade Basin (Mather Pass, 12,000')
Crater Mountain-Mt. Wayne (Pinchot Pass, 12,100')
Mt. Gardiner-Painted Lady Ridge (Glen Pass, 11,980')
Kings-Kern Divide (Forester Pass, 13,200')

Eugene Rose

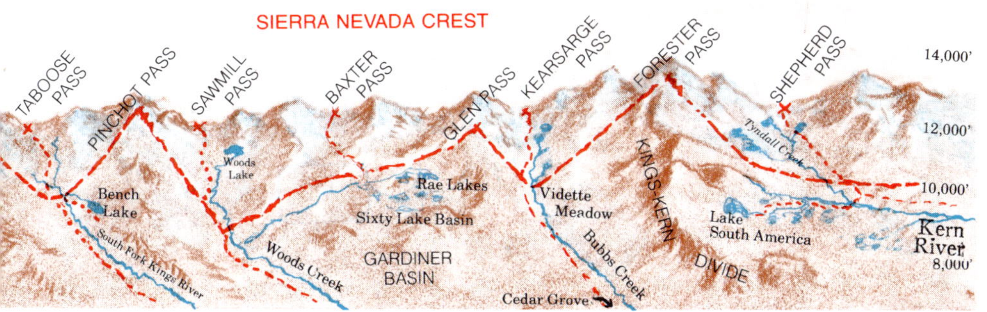

The South Lake-Bishop route leads into the Muir Pass-Goddard Divide region that separates the waters of the southwest-flowing Kings and the northwest-flowing San Joaquin rivers. Most popular of the trips into this area is that connecting North Lake over Piute Pass, down Piute Canyon to the south fork of the San Joaquin, up Evolution Valley through the sublime meadows of McClure and Colby, to the barren alpine lakes and over Muir Pass, down the LeConte Canyon with the most spectacular scenery, to a lovely camping spot at Little Pete Meadow nestled below Langille Peak, up Dusy Creek to the famous Dusy Basin, over the Bishop Pass and down to South Lake. Indeed one of the most exciting ventures of the entire Sierra and which represents the fullness of this range.

From the roadend near South Lake (9800') there is a large parking area for back-country hikers. From there to the Pass it is only seven miles with a moderate climb. Surrounded by towering walls and peaks in a sub-alpine setting the route includes passing Long Lake, Saddlerock, and several smaller ones. Along the way there are many wildflowers in the small meadow area and aspen groves. At the higher elevations the lodgepoles thin out and a few whitebark pine appear before reaching treeline above Saddlerock Lake. The last, short, steep ascent to the Pass is breathtaking in its intimate exposure to the abrupt face of the Sierra Crest between the Palisades and Mt. Darwin – also breathtaking is the exertion needed at this high altitude to propel yourself and your pack to get there. At the pass the view west extends across the tremendous trough of LeConte Canyon to the rugged crest of the Black Divide, and south across the Dusy and Palisades basins of the upper Kings. Just below Dusy Basin the trail descends rapidly to the junction with the John Muir-Pacific Crest Trail in the LeConte Canyon near Little Pete Meadows.

For the hardy hiker, travel can be made into the Barrett Lakes of the Palisade Basin cross-country from the Dusy Lake Basin.

North Lake (9200') – Piute Pass (11,423')

This is the eastern entry into the famous Humphrey's Basin and French Canyon fishing country which are the headwater basins of Piute Creek and the San Joaquin River. The trail up the pass is an easy-grade route through groves of lodgepole and aspen and a profusion of wildflowers in season. Flanked by the towering Mt. Lamarck (13,427') and Mt. Emerson (13,225') Piute Lake adds charm and beauty to this mountain journey. The Wonder Lakes and Lamarck Lakes are an angler's delight with catches of Eastern Brook and Rainbow Trout.

The forty square miles of Humphrey's Basin-French Canyon high country lies entirely within the John Muir Wilderness. Several major streams and some sixty-seven lakes have been planted and managed with the idea of maintaining this region as a home for Golden Trout.

Blue Lake *Rocky Rockwell*

Wanda Lake *Eugene Rose*

MUIR PASS COUNTRY

It is indeed a backpackers or mountain climbers paradise in this Middle Fork of the Kings River Country with tarn-spotted basins; many deep, seldom explored canyons, challenging peaks to scale, and panoramic vistas of breathtaking beauty. A distinctive high country environment is the specialty of this region. At Little Pete Meadows and Evolution Valley are open, flowered meadows sheltered with towering peaks, and full-flowing, sparkling clear streams with camping conditions at their best. Fishing in the tumbling, gurgling Middle Fork down the LeConte Canyon is a glorious mountain activity.

Approaches to the Goddard Divide crossing at Muir Pass (11,955') lead up through a succession of upper valleys and canyons enclosed by almost overwhelming walls and peaks. On the south side are Black Divide and the LeConte Canyon, on the north is the Evolution Basin beneath the massive Darwin Range and to the south the forbidden Ionian Basin. Ridges and peaks surrounding this pass exceed 13,000' elevation. These mighty giants add their majesty as protective guardians to those who traverse this land. It is most fitting that this most awesome, high mountain pass be named after John Muir, the most revered mountain man who explored the Sierra. Nearby Wanda and Helen lakes were named after his two daughters.

The Muir Shelter at the pass was built some years ago by the Sierra Club with the assistance of the Forest Service and a generous donation by the late George F. Schwarz. The use of the building is limited to emergencies only – when sudden afternoon or night storms occur and make the crossing difficult. From Big Pete Meadow to Colby Meadow through the pass, only chemical fuel stoves are allowed as the area is closed to all fires.

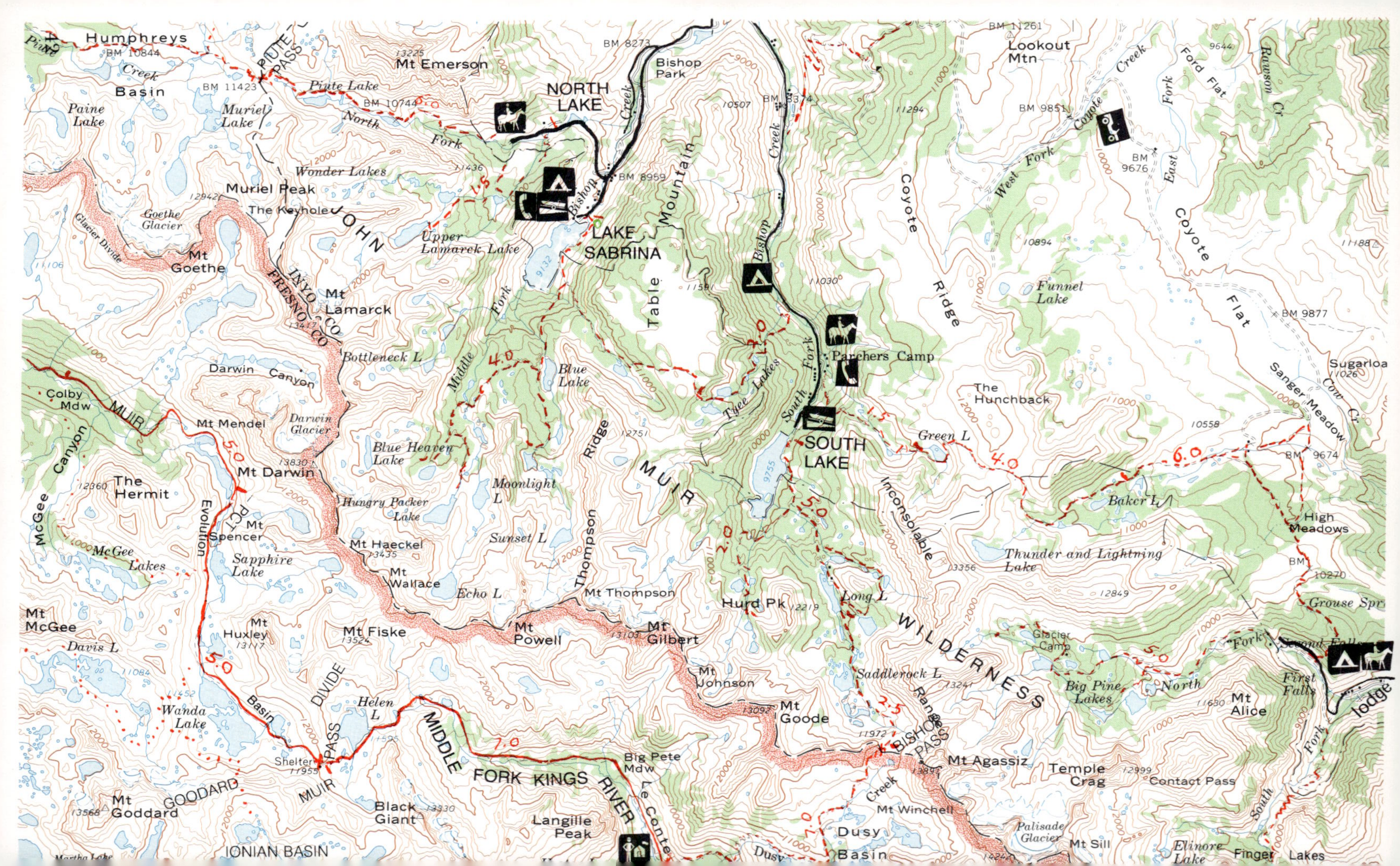

Humphreys
Creek
Basin
Paine Lake
PIUTE PASS
Piute Lake
Muriel Lake
Mt Emerson
NORTH LAKE
Bishop Park
North Fork
Wonder Lakes
Muriel Peak
The Keyhole
JOHN
Goethe Glacier
Glacier Divide
Mt Goethe
Upper Lamarck Lake
LAKE SABRINA
Mountain
Table
INYO CO
FRESNO CO
Mt Lamarck
Bottleneck L
Darwin Canyon
Darwin Glacier
Middle Fork
Blue Lake
Colby Mdw
MUIR
Mt Mendel
Mt Darwin
Blue Heaven Lake
Hungry Packer Lake
Moonlight L
Sunset L
Ridge
Thompson
McGee Canyon
The Hermit
Evolution
PCT
Mt Spencer
Sapphire Lake
McGee Lakes
Mt Haeckel
Mt Wallace
Echo L
Mt Thompson
Mt McGee
Davis L
Mt Huxley
Mt Fiske
Mt Powell
Mt Gilbert
Wanda Lake
Basin
DIVIDE
Helen L
Shelter
MUIR PASS
GOODARD
Mt Goddard
IONIAN BASIN
Black Giant
MIDDLE FORK KINGS RIVER
Big Pete Mdw
Le Conte
Langille Peak
Bishop Creek
South Fork
Tyee Lakes
Parchers Camp
SOUTH LAKE
MUIR
Green L
The Hunchback
Coyote Ridge
Funnel Lake
Lookout Mtn
West Fork
Coyote Creek
East Fork
Ford Flat
Rawson Cr
Coyote Flat
Sanger Meadow
Sugarloa
Cow Cr
Baker L
High Meadows
Inconsolable
Thunder and Lightning Lake
Hurd Pk
Long L
WILDERNESS
Saddlerock L
Range
BISHOP PASS
Mt Johnson
Mt Goode
Mt Agassiz
Mt Winchell
Creek
Dusy Basin
Palisade Glacier
Mt Sill
Glacier Camp
Big Pine Lakes
North Fork
Grouse Spr
Second Falls
First Falls
Mt Alice
Temple Crag
Contact Pass
South Fork
Elinore Lake
Finger Lakes
lodge

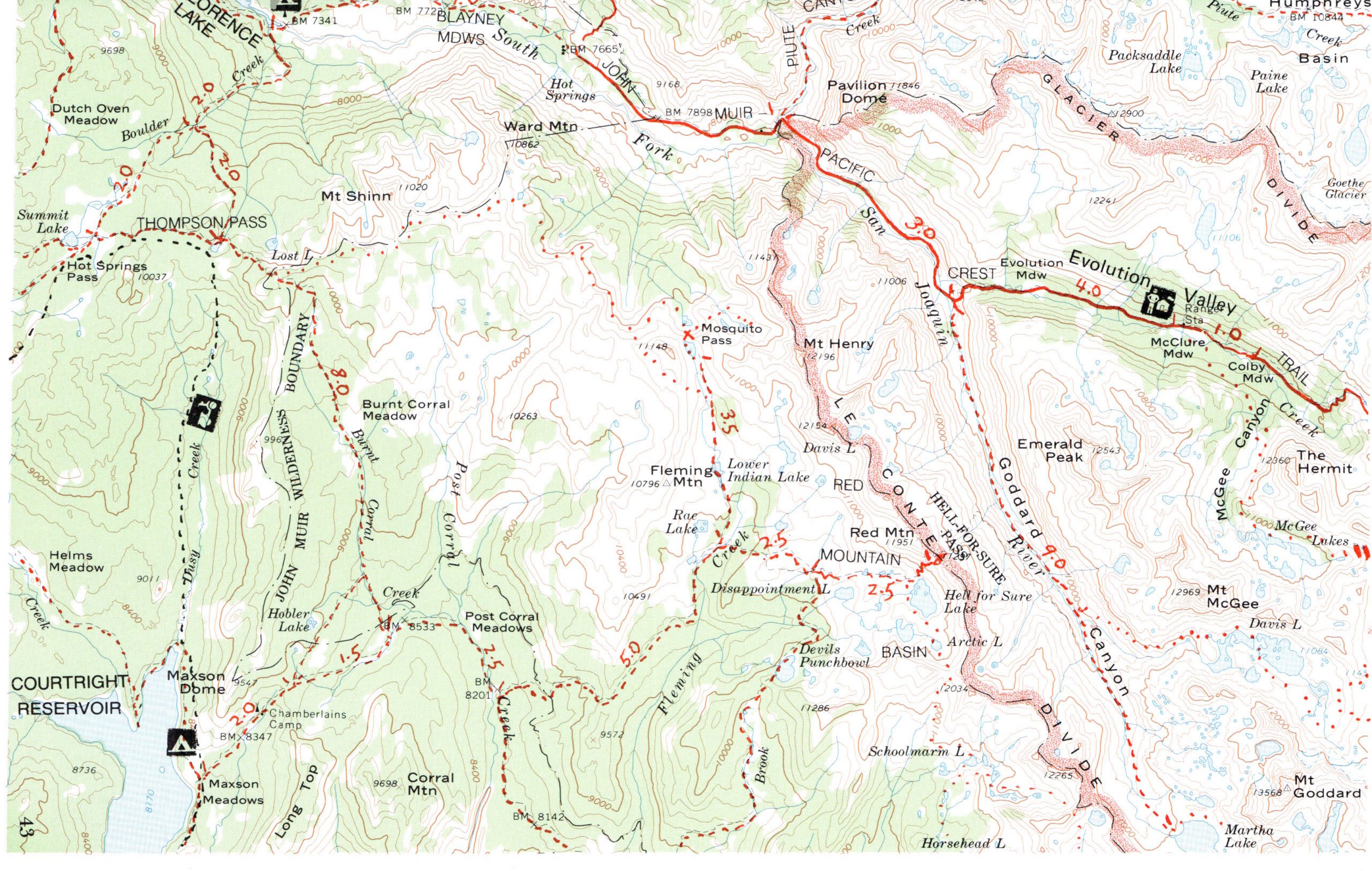

FLORENCE LAKE
BLAYNEY MDWS
South
Hot Springs
JOHN MUIR
Fork
Ward Mtn
PIUTE
Creek
Humphreys
Piute
Basin
Packsaddle Lake
Paine Lake
Pavilion Dome
GLACIER
DIVIDE
Goethe Glacier
PACIFIC
San Joaquin
CREST
Evolution Mdw
Evolution Valley
Ranger Sta
McClure Mdw
Colby Mdw
TRAIL
Dutch Oven Meadow
Boulder
Mt Shinn
Summit Lake
THOMPSON PASS
Hot Springs Pass
Lost L
Mosquito Pass
Mt Henry
Davis L
LE CONTE
RED MOUNTAIN
HELL-FOR-SURE PASS
Goddard River
Canyon
Emerald Peak
McGee Canyon Creek
The Hermit
McGee Lakes
Mt McGee
Davis L
JOHN MUIR WILDERNESS BOUNDARY
Burnt Corral Meadow
Burnt Corral
Post Corral Creek
Post Corral Meadows
Fleming Mtn
Lower Indian Lake
Rae Lake
Red Mtn
Disappointment L
Hell for Sure Lake
Arctic L
BASIN
Devils Punchbowl
Fleming
Brook
Schoolmarm L
DIVIDE
Mt Goddard
Martha Lake
Horsehead L
Helms Meadow
Dusy Creek
Hobler Lake
COURTRIGHT RESERVOIR
Maxson Dome
Chamberlains Camp
Maxson Meadows
Long Top
Corral Mtn
Creek

WESTERN APPROACHES

The shortest and easiest route into the headwaters of the Middle Fork of the Kings is via a boat ride or easy walk to the headwaters of Florence Lake. Although presently dammed, it was a natural lake. From there the trail leads up the South Fork of the San Joaquin River to Blayney Meadows, up Evolution Valley, over the Muir Pass to LeConte Canyon and beyond. A trail leads south from Florence Lake over Thompson Pass (9600') to the North Fork of the Kings River.

The road from Kaiser Crest east of Huntington Lake to Florence Lake, though partly paved, is an almost one-way road and could be a hairy, yet interesting ride if unfamiliar with mountain driving. (Uphill drivers have the right-of-way.) Large RV units and trailers are definitely not advised as sharp curves and dropoffs make it difficult to see approaching vehicles.

At Florence Lake there is a corral for pack trips into the North Fork of the Kings Country as well as into the vast Bear Creek and Mono Creek fishing country. There is a campground, backcountry parking and a store with limited supplies.

At Piute Canyon, the John Muir-Pacific Crest Trail follows up the U-shaped canyon walls of the San Joaquin River, crossing a suspended bridge before it junctions with the Goddard Canyon trail to Martha Lake. One of the most spectacular gorges in all of the Kings Canyon National Park is up the Goddard Creek with the steep canyon wall of the LeConte Divide, the numerous waterfalls, and the desolate alpine scenery. On the cross-country trail to Davis Lakes area avoid the precipitous ascent around the falls by staying somewhat away from the North Goddard Creek. A basecamp is located at Martha Lake, one of the most beautiful high mountain lakes, for climbers of Mt. Goddard. The trail is not maintained yet it is passable.

There are three large meadows in Evolution Valley where camping is available before ascending into the upper Muir Pass country. Be sure to check for availability of camping sites as this is a very popular area.

Evolution Valley with The Hermit *NPS Photo*

THE NORTH FORK OF THE KINGS COUNTRY

The headwaters of the North Fork of the Kings are found along the western slopes of the LeConte-White Divide. Ancient glacial activity carved out scores of basins now separated by low, forested hills. Today, most of it lies within the John Muir Wilderness. Its western sloping exposure of pine and fir forests have long been enjoyed by family campers, backpackers, and anglers. Red Mountain Basin, Upper Fleming Creek, Bench Valley, Blackcap Basin, Crown Valley, Woodchuck Country and the Dinkey Creek Lakes Country are all unique in their geologic setting and exceptional fishing. Principal entry points into these areas are Shaver Lake, Huntington Lake, Florence Lake, and the Wishon and Courtright Reservoirs trailheads.

The Thompson Pass trail to the North Fork proceeds into the John Muir Wilderness where the elevations are lower, with more meadows and forest cover than the rugged granite canyons and glacial basins of the Middle Fork country. Fishing is great and the weather ideal with well maintained trails and wonderful camping available.

From Thompson Pass, a good cross-country trip can be made to the Upper Fleming Creek Lakes, Red Mountain Basin and return via the North Fork of the Kings and Burnt Corral trails. The trail (unmarked on map) from Ward Mountain down to Blaney Meadows is extremely rough and the crossing of the South Fork of the San Joaquin River there is hazardous and not advised when the waters are high.

Much of the upper country of the Red Mountain-Fleming Creek basin lies in a high country, granitoid, glacial setting, some above timberline where wood is scarce. Here chemical fuel stoves are needed for overnight camps. Below timberline the common forest cover is lodgepole pine and red fir, while juniper and whitebark pine appear in decreasing numbers at higher elevations. The Upper Fleming Creek Basin below Mosquito Pass (10,500') is great fishing country in both streams and lakes which support Rainbow and Eastern Brook trout. From Hell-For-Sure Lake (10,803'), which dominates the Red Mountain basin, the steep trail to the pass with rocky switchbacks is a pull, but well worth it with the view of the deep-walled Goddard Canyon, Emerald and McGee peaks standing guard above. In some seasons the snow stays until late summer in some of the canyons. The trail from Hell-For-Sure Pass down to Goddard Canyon is now discontinued.

From the upper San Joaquin River basin there are several choices of trans-Sierra routes which offer a wide range of great camping experiences with the finest scenery and excellent fishing. The Florence Lake to North Lake of Bishop Creek Basin follows from Blayney Meadow, up Piute Creek into Humphrey's Basin, over Piute Pass and down to North Lake. For those who would enjoy combining an old Indian trail with a section of "high" Sierra along the John Muir-Pacific Crest Trail, consider the route from Florence Lake, up Evolution Valley, over Muir Pass, down to Grouse Meadow, up over Bishop Pass, down to South Lake of Bishop Creek Basin.

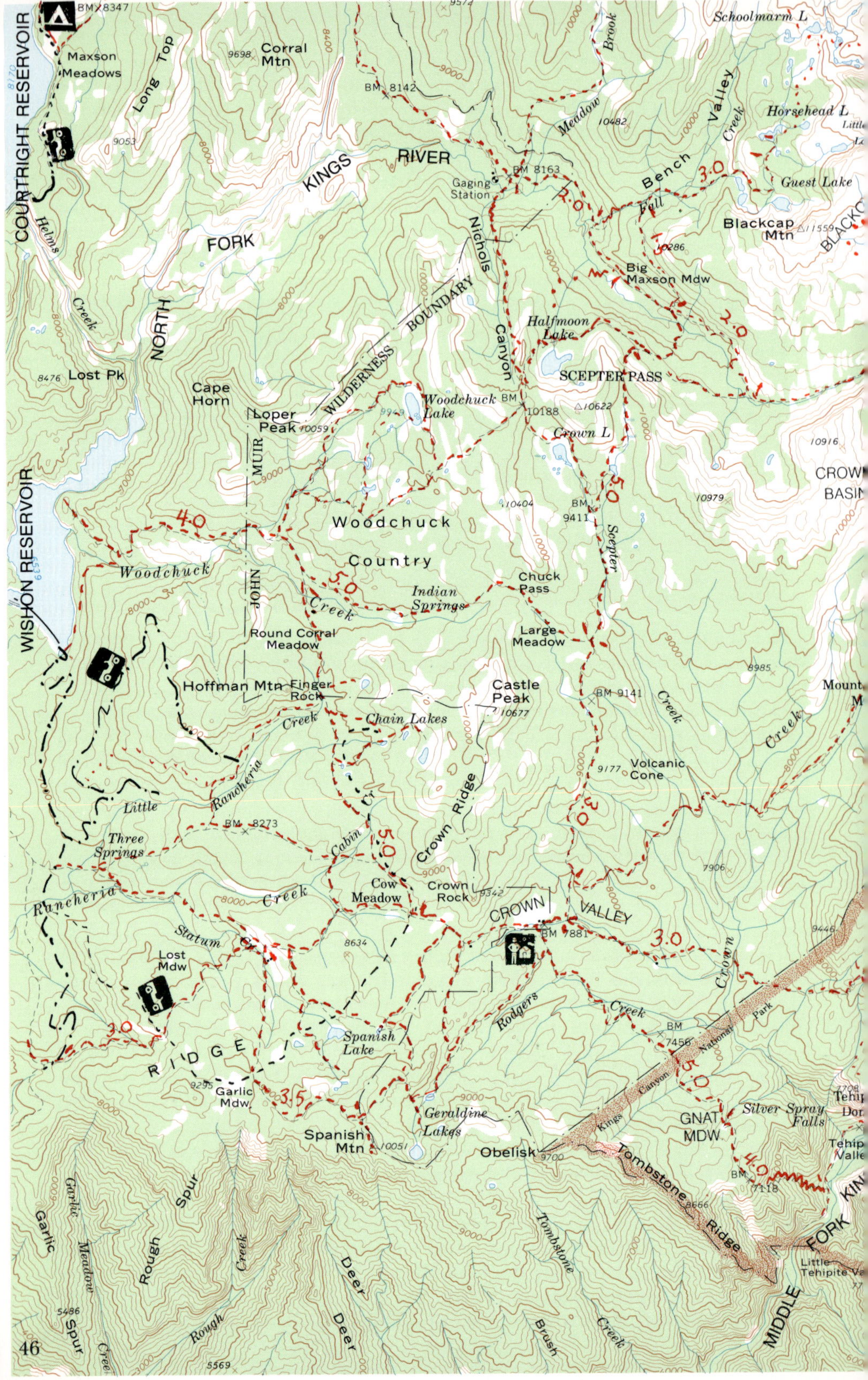
COURTRIGHT RESERVOIR
Maxson Meadows
Long Top
Corral Mtn
Schoolmarm L
Brook
Meadow
Horsehead L
Valley
Creek
KINGS
RIVER
Gaging Station
Bench
Fall
Guest Lake
Blackcap Mtn
Helms
FORK
Nichols
Big Maxson Mdw
WILDERNESS
BOUNDARY
Halfmoon Lake
Creek
NORTH
Canyon
SCEPTER PASS
Lost Pk
Cape Horn
Woodchuck Lake
Loper Peak
Crown L
MUIR
CROWN BASIN
WISHON RESERVOIR
Woodchuck
Country
Scepter
Woodchuck
JOHN
Indian Springs
Chuck Pass
Creek
Round Corral Meadow
Large Meadow
Hoffman Mtn
Finger Rock
Castle Peak
Chain Lakes
Volcanic Cone
Little
Rancheria
Crown Ridge
Three Springs
Cabin
Cr
Cow Meadow
Crown Rock
CROWN
VALLEY
Rancheria
Creek
Statum
Lost Mdw
Rodgers
Creek
Crown
Spanish Lake
RIDGE
Garlic Mdw
Geraldine Lakes
Spanish Mtn
Obelisk
Kings Canyon National Park
GNAT MDW
Silver Spray Falls
Tombstone
Ridge
Garlic
Meadow
Spur
Rough
Creek
Deer
Tombstone
Brush
Creek
MIDDLE
FORK
KINGS
Little Tehipite Va

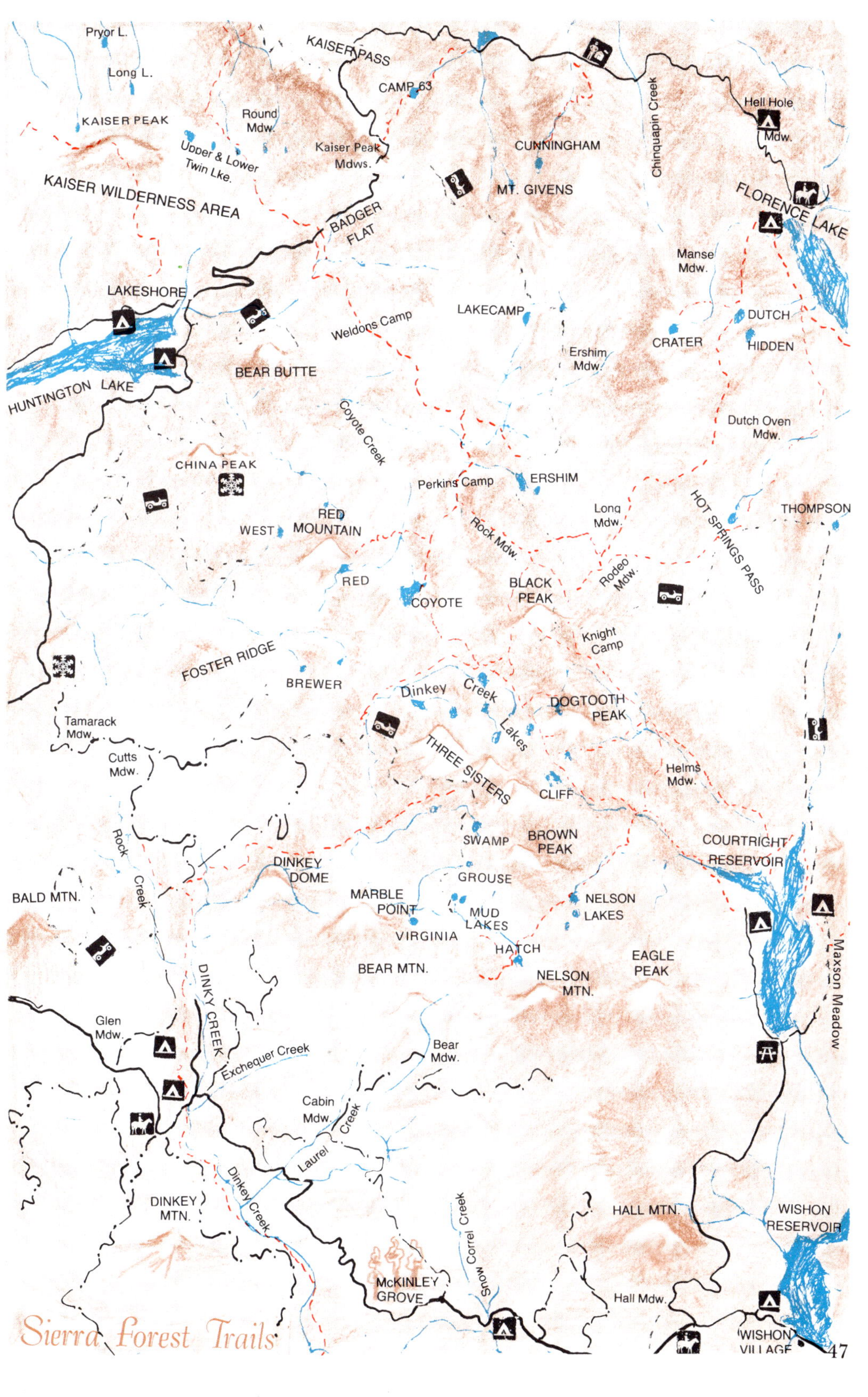

Pryor L.
Long L.
KAISER PASS
CAMP 63
KAISER PEAK
Round Mdw.
Upper & Lower Twin Lke.
Kaiser Peak Mdws.
KAISER WILDERNESS AREA
BADGER FLAT
CUNNINGHAM
MT. GIVENS
Chinquapin Creek
Hell Hole Mdw.
FLORENCE LAKE
Manse Mdw.
LAKESHORE
HUNTINGTON LAKE
Weldons Camp
LAKECAMP
BEAR BUTTE
Ershim Mdw.
CRATER
DUTCH
HIDDEN
Coyote Creek
Dutch Oven Mdw.
CHINA PEAK
Perkins Camp
ERSHIM
RED MOUNTAIN
WEST
Long Mdw.
HOT SPRINGS PASS
THOMPSON
Rock Mdw.
Rodeo Mdw.
RED
COYOTE
BLACK PEAK
Knight Camp
FOSTER RIDGE
BREWER
Dinkey Creek Lakes
DOGTOOTH PEAK
Tamarack Mdw.
Cutts Mdw.
THREE SISTERS
Helms Mdw.
CLIFF
Rock Creek
SWAMP
BROWN PEAK
COURTRIGHT RESERVOIR
DINKEY DOME
GROUSE
BALD MTN.
MARBLE POINT
NELSON LAKES
MUD LAKES
VIRGINIA
HATCH
EAGLE PEAK
BEAR MTN.
NELSON MTN.
Maxson Meadow
DINKY CREEK
Glen Mdw.
Exchequer Creek
Bear Mdw.
Cabin Mdw.
Laurel Creek
Dinkey Creek
DINKEY MTN.
Snow Correl Creek
HALL MTN.
WISHON RESERVOIR
McKINLEY GROVE
Hall Mdw.
WISHON VILLAGE
Sierra Forest Trails

SHAVER – HUNTINGTON TRAILHEAD

The North Fork of the Kings River and its main tributaries such as Helms Creek and the most westerly – Dinkey Creek has its origin along the southern heights of the Foster Ridge-Black Peak highland. Helms Creek flows into Courtright and down into Wishon (where the Pacific Gas and Electric Company project is located). The Dinkey Lakes lie in a horseshoe basin rimmed by Nelson Mountain, Brown Peak, Three Sisters, Dogtooth Peak, Black Peak, and to the west Foster Ridge. In this basin the low ridges provide an excellent setting for many lakes. ponds, and streams connecting them. It is an ideal place for beginners or family camping whether they plan to fish, take pictures, or just sit around the campfire in the great out-of-doors.

Most of the fish are Eastern Brook that do unusually well in these meadow-lined waters. The California Fish & Game Department administers the fish planting and studies the angling conditions to insure a fair catch with a good replenishment program.

This region is well forested with pine, fir, cedar, and such broadleaved trees as oak, maple, alder, and cottonwood. In suitable areas are found juniper, aspen, and laurel. There is a nice group of sequoias at McKinley Grove about five miles southeast of Dinkey Creek on the road to Wishon. The multiple-use ethics of the U.S. Forest Service is well illustrated in this area. Efforts are made to maintain a balance between the uses of trees for lumber or shelter for wildlife and campers, between grassy meadows for stock or wildflowers for summer visitors, and between water for irrigation and power and/or recreational activities – all of this within a consistent pattern with the natural environment.

Access to this region can be made at Shaver Lake or Huntington Lake. There is a long, winding road up from Sanger to Pine Flat Reservoir, Balch Camp, Black Rock Station and to Wishon Reservoir. The Clovis-Shaver Lake-Dinkey Creek route to both Wishon and Courtright is the preferred route.

Shaver Lake has every convenience a camper or backpacker could need. There are campgrounds and excellent lake fishing all the year round. There are campgrounds at Dinkey Creek, Courtright and Wishon reservoirs, as well as pack stations for day or extended backcountry travel. At Wishon Village there is a trailer park with full hook-ups, improved campsites, cafe, bar, and boat rentals. They are open from May 1st to November 1st. Motors are allowed on the lake with a speed of 15 mph but no water skiing. There are showers, laundry facilities, gas, ice, propane, and complete tackle supplies at the store. From Shaver Lake it is approximately twenty-nine miles to Wishon Village.

WISHON-COURTRIGHT RESERVOIRS TRAILHEAD

The Sierra is a friendly place inviting entry at all seasons. Its extensive, striking geology along the high eastern crest has, since early days, excited the interest of scholars and mountaineers. For decades the goal of vacationers has been the High Sierra. The term has become synonymous with any place in the mountains above the oak tree and digger pine belt. The almost revered regard Californians have had about this granite crest has created a problem of serious magnitude as visitations increased from a few hundred to several million in a single summer. Strangely enough the corridor region named to give honor to John Muir traverses an area he seldom visited. Most of his journeys were an up canyon-down canyon course exploring the rivers and their source. Of special concern to him were the deep grassy valleys and meadows that supported a complete spectrum of wildlife.

The country that lies along the west slope of the crest of the LeConte-White Divide where rain, snow, and deep soil have developed an abundance of trees, streams, and wildlife has some of the finest camping with wood, water and great fishing.

COURTRIGHT BASIN – BLACKCAP BASIN (approx. 25 miles) For Blackcap Basin see map page 23.)

Route follows up the North Fork of the Kings via Post Corral Meadows, down to Big Maxson Meadow to the Blackcap basin. In these headwaters the California Fish and Game lists more than sixty lakes and streams, most of them above 10,000'. Eastern Brooks and Rainbow have been planted and a few lakes at the higher elevations contain Goldens. Peaks of the LeConte Divide and Kettle Ridge form a splendid skyline show at daybreak. At this hour the wind is low and the deep blue lakes reflect the jagged peaks.

The trail follows along the reservoir about a mile, then goes east into Woodchuck Country and Halfmoon Lake, over Scepter Pass (9400') to Blackcap Basin. There is an extensive forested region west of the lakes, scattered groves to timberline that provide good camping, but have a chemical fuel stove for cooking as wood can be scarce anywhere above 9500' level.

Tehipite Dome *NPS Photo*

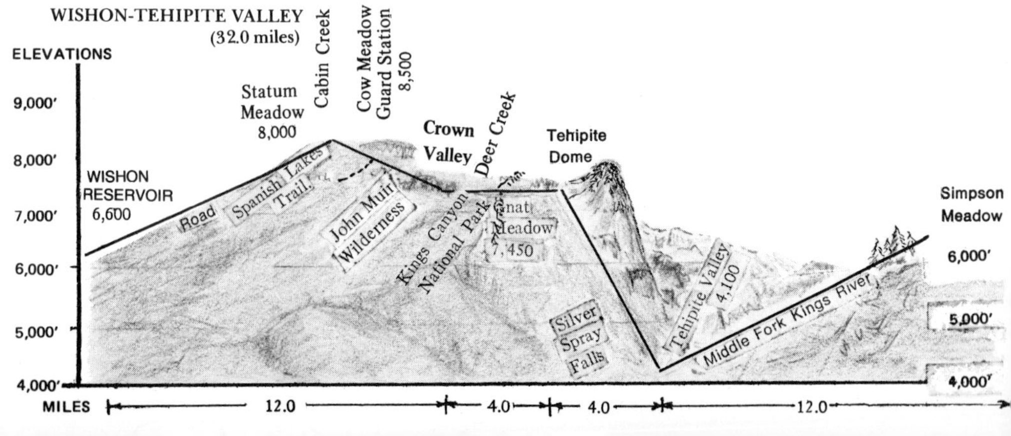

WOODCHUCK COUNTRY

From the Wishon Dam this route is a continuous eight mile climb all the way to Woodchuck. The entire region welcomes camping with its gentle, partly forested hills and meadow-bordered lakes. To the south and east is found some of the finest stands of lodegpole pine, mountain hemlock, and red and white fir. Here and there partially bare ridges lend contrast to the deep green woods and blue skies. It is the habitat of many forest creatures. The traveler is apt to find mule deer, skunk, squirrels, porcupine, bear as well as many birds – blue jay, junco, nuthatch and robin. Shooting stars, mariposa lily and mountain aster bloom abundantly in the meadows.

Fishing is excellent. Woodchuck Lake, nestled in between two almost bald ridges, has meadows above and below it and supports a good sized Eastern Brook. The smaller Chimney Lake at a lightly lower elevation also carries Brooks. At the head of Scepter Creek the meadow rimmed Crown Lake produces Rainbow. There is good stream fishing in both Woodchuck and Scepter creeks that carry Rainbow and Eastern Brook.

WISHON-TEHIPITE VALLEY (Middle Fork of the Kings) – SIMPSON MEADOW

The route follows south from Wishon to Crown Valley entering Kings Canyon National Park near Gnat Meadows, then descending some 3550' to the river via a series of switchbacks just west of Tehipite Dome. Under forested cover of lodgepole, jeffrey, incense cedar and white fir with meadows of lupine, larkspur and monkey flower, jeep roads and trails lead to Crown Valley from Wishon Reservoir. It is excellent horseback-riding country and the duff on the trail is easier to take from the height of a horse than mere walking through it. In the late, dry season the grazing of cattle creates dust.

An interesting side trip from Crown Valley is to follow up Rodgers Creek to Spanish Mountain (10,051'). Rodgers Ridge separates the North Fork of the Kings River with the South Fork. From this peak one can look down the highest canyon wall of some 8000' to the river far below. An awesome sight indeed!

CROWN VALLEY – TEHIPITE VALLEY – SIMPSON MEADOW (21.0 miles)

At Gnat Meadow take time to explore the rim area to the east for an excellent view of the Tehipite Dome and the great canyon wall of the Middle Fork to the south.

Following the trail to Gnat Meadows and the Tehipite Valley trail, it is 9.0 miles to the river. Overnight camping is available at Gnat Meadow (also know as Hay Meadow) before descending the rough switchbacks to the river. There are no camping places along the Middle Fork of the Kings to Simpson Meadow.

The valley floor is small and rough with the canyon walls close to the river. Crown Creek comes tumbling down over cascades and becomes the Silver Spray Falls to join the Middle Fork. Tehipite Dome is truly a shape of beauty and is a most predominate and impressive dome. Parts of the trail up the Middle Fork to Simpson Meadow are very rough, especially along the close canyon walls.

CROWN VALLEY – BLUE CANYON – TUNEMAH TRAIL – SIMPSON-MEADOW (25.0 miles)

In the early days this trail was used by the sheepherders and cattlemen to reach the grazing at Simpson Meadow. From Blue Canyon it is a cross-country trail crossing below the White Divide just above Burnt Mountain as shown on map page 23.

At Kettle Dome there is a good, short cross-country trail for those wishing to climb the top of Tehipite Dome. From the top the view is tremendous, with the majestic south wall of the Monarch Divide and with the pinnacle-shaped Kennedy Mountain, Hogbeck Peak, the avalanche shutes and Slide Peak.

The steep trail descending into Blue Canyon east of Kettle Dome (shown on map page 23) is rocky with some forest cover and wildflowers along the trail. The good camping area and the availability of firewood makes this area a great wilderness experience.

NATURE NOTES

THE SIERRAN LAND

There is good evidence that the Sierra Nevada was not over-ridden by the vast continental glaciers, but rather the development was of regional glacial activity at a more recent time in more scattered patterns where special conditions fostered their growth.

Some ice fields and streams flowed east or west as on the NW and SE patterns. Terminal moraines are found adjacent to the east face of the Sierra rampart where desert sage now flourish. American valleys formed by alternative folding and stream action became subjected to glacial forces that were apt to be denied until they reached the lower melting-level elevations.

The full enjoyment of the Sierra Nevada is enlarged as the traveler becomes involved with all its aspects. It is a land of great contrasts with its towering peaks and deep valleys, its lush mountain meadows and alpine plateaus, its giant sequoias and its alpine willows, and its roaring torrents whose waters began in quiet glacial pools along the skyline crest.

Since John Muir's reporting in 1894 of glacial effects on the southern Sierra much has been added to our knowledge of their action as found along the Sierra crest. In deeply shaded northern slopes, they continue their activities of *plucking* and *quarrying* great blocks of granite, then transporting them to lower elevations to eventually become embedded in terminal or lateral moraines or left isolated as *erratics* in some unconventional setting.

The run-off from glacial rivlets and streams becomes colored with the milky-white glacial flour as ancient, impregnable granite mountains are reduced to become the top soil of mountain meadows. In their small way they provide another type of outdoor museum for our study of the great forces of nature that produced the Kern Canyon or the Kings Canyon wonderland.

Over the short space of some sixty to seventy miles between the dry, oak and chaparral foothills and the snow-capped Sierra crest, climatic and food types supporting birds and animals are as extensive as those resulting changing conditions that cover the wide range of western America lying between the southwestern desert and the northern arctic tundra regions almost 2,000 miles to the north. The visitor, in a space of a few days, and sometimes in a few hours, will cross many physical life zones.

Most regions have a fairly stable weather situation developing from a typical elevation and latitude condition. Elevation alone, although significant, is not a sole definitive determinant. The usual maps and diagrams are not a literal definition of boundary lines, only general indications as to where changes can probably be expected.

Life zones are a reflection of weather belts where there is a reasonable consistency of certain shrubs and trees suitable to the shelter and food supply for its wildlife. Zones can change along the trail when trying to identify wildlife as there are a few general conditions that uniformly encourage birds and animals to seek a certain area: (1) adequate food supply; (2) appropriate cover providing refuge from natural enemies; (3) suitable nesting conditions; (4) climatic conditions appropriate to their needs; and (5) special survival abilities and habits such as migration, adaptation, and hibernation. The last condition is especially important to such animals as deer, cony, and alpine chipmunk. Each choose their own specialized form of survival with the change of season.

Eugene Rose

The Sierran region follows the weather and life zone pattern only as it relates to southern and northern areas. A venture into the Sierra either west or east produces dramatic changes in weather, plant life, and the wildlife. At times backcountry adventurers will experience dramatic changes in a matter of a few hours when traveling routes across the Sierra. Some routes, however, follow deep canyons or broad plateaus for many miles before exhibiting significant zonal differences.

On the western slope climate and soil conditions have developed consistent type plant-belts: the dry foothills supporting grasses, chaparral, and oaks; the great forest regions made up of mostly pines and firs; and the higher Sierran plateaus and divides where soil and climatic conditions are the most difficult for plant survival. In the Lower-Transition and Sonoran zones will be found broadleaved oaks, alders, buckeye, manzanita; quail and many birds; the ring-tailed cat, raccoon, skunk, and squirrels, with a profusion of flowers. The forested, higher Canadian and Lower-Hudsonian zones have conifers, azalea, deer, bear, many squirrels and chipmunks, pine marten and birds. In the Hudsonian-Alpine zones live the cony, rosy finch, marmot, foxtail and whitebark pines, and such hardy plants as the sky pilot, Alpine buttercup, Sierra primrose, and the Alpine willow. Here in the arctic-alpine region the weather is acceptable to only the most rugged, especially adapted shrubs and even these are in limited numbers.

The east slope of the Sierra is so abrupt between the Owens Valley and the Sierra crest adjacent to it that climatic conditions are not as consistent with changes in elevation as on the west. Here will be found a general intermingling, cosmopolitan arrangement of both plant and animal life except at the extreme elevations. All life as well as climate is compressed into such a limited space that definite separations do not exist. Trees are not as tall and usually grow quite scattered from one another to secure adequate food supply in the soil and moisture. Vegetation may range between desert-like sagebrush flats to sub-alpine hills in the course of three to four hours walking. Even the wildlife gives a special character to the region, such as the pinyon pine, extensive groups of Jeffrey pines, antelope ground squirrel, and the mountain sheep.

IDENTIFYING THE MOST COMMON CONE-BEARING TREES

NAME	SILHOUETTE	CONES	BARK	NEEDLES	RESIDENCE PREFERENCE
PONDEROSA PINE	100′–180′ ht. 3′–5′ dia. Trunk smooth, cylindrical, with little taper until crown branches. Limbs tip upward on ends.	2¾″–5¾″ long. 2″–3″ dia. Oval shape, clustered near end of branches.	3″–4″ thick. Surface divided into broad, shieldlike yellow plates. Surface broken into small, concave, flaky scales.	6″–11¼″ long. 3 in a bundle. Deep yellow-green. Grouped in heavy, brushlike clusters at ends of branches.	3,000′–5,500′ elevations. (*Transition.*) Very wide distribution.
INCENSE-CEDAR	75′–120′ ht. 2¼′–4½′ dia. Crown open and irregular on mature trees. Young have smooth, conical shape.	1″–1½″ long. ½″ dia. Urn-shaped when green. Sections roll back when ripe.	3″–8″ thick on mature trees. Cinnamon-red, deeply fissured with soft, stringy texture. On young trees is thin, scaly, reddish-brown, flakes off easily.	¼″–½″ scalelike leaves covering twigs in tight, overlapping sequence. Very fragrant. Rich, shiny-green coloring	3,000′–6,000′ elevation. (*Transition.*) Some are 5′–6′ dia. and 125–150′ ht. Those 2′–3′ dia. approx. 300 yrs. A few reach 500 yrs.
SUGAR PINE	150′–200′ ht. 5′–8′ dia. Flat-topped, long sweeping branches in upper third of tree.	12″–23″ long. 2½″–5″ dia. Pendent near outer ends of upper branches.	1½″–4″ thick. Medium brown, deeply fissured segments tinged with red.	2½″–4″ long. 5 in a bundle. Blue-green.	4,000′–8,000′ elevation. (*Transition & Canadian.*) North and east slopes of canyons
WHITE FIR	140′–180′ ht. 3½′–6′ dia. Very massive. Lower 1/3 clear.	3″–5″ long. 1½″–2¾″ dia. Erect on outer tips of limbs near top of trees.	4″–6½″ thick. Silvery on young trees. Ash-gray to deep brownish-yellow beneath. Young stems have resin blisters.	1″–3″ long. Longest of any fir. Stands out from branch with a twist at its base. Green with whitish tinge.	3,500′–8,000′ elevation. (*Transition into Canadian.*) 3½′–5′ dia. trees range from 275–450 yrs. old.
RED FIR	125′–175′ ht. 1½′–5′ dia. Many with broken crowns.	5″–8″ long. 2¾″–3½″ dia. Stand erect near tips of branches. Purplish, edged with brown.	2″–5″ thick. Deeply fissured and divided by short, diagonal ridges. Outer scales dark red. Inner segments bright red. Surface rough.	¾″–1¼″ long. Four-sided, rounded on top. Attached directly to stem. Limbs form heavy sprays in whorl formation.	6,000′–9,000′ elevation. (*Canadian.*) Trees 20″–30″ dia. average 225–375 yrs. old.
WESTERN WHITE PINE	**50' - 120' ht. Tall, straight, gently tapered trunk. Upper limbs outward and upward. Similar to Sugar Pine.**	**4" - 10" long. Slender, hang from tips of branches.**	**1" thick. Surface divided into almost square plates. Dark gray, few loose scales.**	**2" - 3½" long. 5 in a bundle. Slender, green. Little shorter than Sugar Pine.**	**5,500' - 7,500'. (Canadian.) Found on Alta Peak Trail and Monarch Divide Country.**

JEFFREY PINE	125′–175′ ht. 1½′–4½′ dia. Rounded top and many limbs. Large-bodied and straight.	5″–11″ long. 3″–6″ dia. Purplish cast.	1½″–3″ thick. Reddish-brown, broken into deep plates by narrow furrows. Strong vanilla or pineapple odor.	7″–11″ long. 3 in bundle. Blue-green coloring.	5,500′–8,500′ elevation. (*Canadian.*) Some age up to 400 yrs. Becomes stunted in high, rocky areas.
MOUNTAIN HEMLOCK	25′–100′ ht. 1′–3½′ dia. Limbs close to ground.	1″–3″ long. ½″–1½″ dia. Abundant near top.	Young trees: thin and silvery. Mature trees: 1¼″ thick, reddish-brown, deeply ridged and furrowed.	½″–¾″ long. Grows spirally around branches. Appear thicker on upper side.	7,700′ on up the cool, northern slopes to timberline. Trees 18″–20″ dia. and 50′–60′ ht. reach ages of 180–250 yrs.
SIERRA JUNIPER	10′–30′ ht. 3′–6′ dia. Heavy, twisted trunk.	¼″–½″ dia. Looks more like berry than a cone. Divided into three sections. Covered with whitish bloom. Very pungent odor.	2½″–5″ thick. Reddish-brown. Long, fibrous ridges of soft bark is easily stripped from trunk.	⅛″ long. Scalelike, overlapping in clusters of three, similar to incense-cedar. Gray-green.	6,500′–10,000′ elevation. (*Canadian & Hudsonian.*) On rocky hillsides. Older trees reach ages 500–1,500 yrs. High, rocky ridges
LODGEPOLE PINE	30′–80′ ht. 1′–2½′ dia. Twisted trunks, often lightning scarred.	1½″–2½″ long. 1″–2″ dia. Very numerous.	Very thin. Light gray and yellowish-brown. Very scaly.	1″–2½″ long. 2 needles in a bundle. Yellowish-green, often twisted.	6,000′–10,000′ elevation. (*Canadian & Hudsonian.*) Ages 100–175 yrs. common.
FOXTAIL PINE	**30' - 40' ht. 3' - 5' dia. Stands erect. Stout, short branches. Weather-beaten. Some dead limbs.**	**2½" - 5" long. Dark brown. Finger-shaped. Incurved prickles.**	**Divided into broad plates. Young trees light gray, smooth. Mature are brown. Old trees orange-brown, furrowed. Lightning scarred.**	**1" - 1¼" long. 5 in a bundle. Dark blue-green. Short, thickly clustered.**	**9,000' to timberline. (Hudsonian.) Found on granite ridges.**
WHITEBARK PINE	15′–40′ ht., 15″–30″ dia. in sheltered areas. On open ridges a sprawling, prostrate, shrublike growth.	1¼″–3½″ long. 1″–2″ dia. Oval-shape. Pitchy, thick scales. Purplish.	⅜″ thick at base to ¼″ on limbs. Dark gray on mature trunk blending to whitish on smooth, outer limbs.	1¼″–2¾″ long. 5 in bundle. Dark, yellow-green and thickly clustered near ends of branches.	9,000′ to timberline. (*Hudsonian.*) 18″–20″ dia. are up to 300 yrs. old. 3½″–4″ dia. may be 250 yrs. old.

BROADLEAVED TREES AND SHRUBS

The gay, fluttering QUAKING ASPEN are water lovers and can be found in groves along streams between 6000' to 10,000' elevation. Their slim trunks grow to a height of 20' to 40'. The bark often indicates the scratch marks of passing animals or thoughtless humans. Their light green leaves, undercoated with silvery-white waver in the slightest breeze. In the autumn they come into their own special glory when they present their great show in the high mountains when the graceful groups turn to gold, orange, and yellow masses of color.

The WILLOW FAMILY loves water. They are found in both bush and tree forms that grow along streams from the foothills to the highest meadows. The slender, limber branches bearing narrow pale-green leaves shade the trout nearby and make nesting shelter for birds.

The ALPINE WILLOW grows beyond the last whitebark pine in moist snow-fed tundra sending forth its limbs in matted patterns just under the surface. It presents its blooms with tiny, 2" tall catkins with a few narrow dark green leaves to protect and encourage its efforts of survival in such a difficult environment.

The CALIFORNIA BLACK OAK is the west's largest oak. This is a 30'-70', deciduous tree with very dark bark, checked into small plates. Leaves are large, 2½" to 6" with three lobes either side, and they put forth great color in the fall. Its rich brown, deep-cut acorns were used by Indians as a main food suply.

Many foothill tree residents prefer the dry slopes, including the CALIFORNIA BUCKEYE which bears erect plumes of small, snowy-white blossoms and green, pear-shaped pods. These seeds, off the tree are very poisonous, but were used by Indians only after grinding and leaching very carefully. Seen along the Generals Highway.

The WESTERN AZALEA, 3'-10', is a moisture-loving shrub with beautiful white blossoms tinged with pink, 1½"-2" long. Leaves are 1" to 4" long. They are found near streams and are very common in the General Grant Grove.

DEER BRUSH, or Ceanothus, or "Wild Lilac" has a delicate, pyramidal spiked white or blue flower. It is a member of the Buckthorn family, and is found on hillsides creating dense coverage for birds and small animals. It blooms in the spring. The leaves are sticky and dark green. The bush grows up to five feet tall.

Other species of Ceanothus are the SIERRA SNOWBRUSH with a white, sweet-smelling flower found from 5000' to 10,000'. The BUCK BRUSH with similar blossoms have smaller leaves than the Deer Brush. This species also gives shelter and provides nest sites for birds. The bark and roots were used in earlier times for home remedies.

The MANZANITA ("Little apple" in Spanish) is an evergreen varying in height from 5" to 6" to several feet, depending on species and locality. It has very hardwood limbs that grow in twisted, distorted patterns. Its deep, red limbs are contrasted by its gray-green leaves, and white urn-shaped flowers. The green and reddish berries resemble small apples and were used by the pioneers to make jelly.

The LABRADOR TEA belongs to the Heath Family. It is a low bush that grows in high elevations, found in boggy places near streams and lakes. The umbrel cluster of small white flowers has a bitter odor when blooming. Tea was made from the green leaves which thickly coat the stem of the plant. It was good for rheumatism.

The CHINQUAPIN selects rocky slopes of forested areas. This shrub has smooth, brown bark, oblong leaves 1½" to 3" long. Their tiny flowers in dense spikes turn into sticky burrs with a chestnut-like seed.

The MOUNTAIN DOGWOOD needs little direct sunlight as their photosynthesis process operates on much less sunlight than most broadleaved trees and shrubs. It grows to heights of 10' to 40' with slender, willowy trunk covered by smooth, grayish to reddish bark. The flowers are actually not the large white petal-like bracts but the small button-like cluster in the center. Dogwood lives modestly in close association with the large pines and conifers seeking their shade during the hot summers and the protection from violent winter storms.

WILD ROSE is very common and found in meadows from 6000' to 8000'. It is a ragged, scraggly shrub with lovely pink blossoms in the early summer. The rich perfume attracts many butterflies and bees. By fall the fruit becomes red berries and the leaves turn from a deep green to a rich reddish-brown.

MOUNTAIN MISERY, or Bear Clover, is 1'-5½' high, with leafy branches on erect, smooth bark. Leaves are dark brown, 3/4" to 4" long, that feel sticky. White, strawberry-like flowers appear in small clusters on the ends of branches The bush smells like creosote when crushed, and sometimes is used for medicine.

GRASSLANDS

Grasslands cover the mountain meadows, and grasses make a cover under the pines and firs in the forests, and can be found in the rocky, talus, alpine slopes as well as under the dry sagebrush and junipers on the eastern slopes. They are a staple food for grasshoppers, squirrels, insects, marmots, rabbits, and mice. Birds eat the seeds. The larger animals prey on the smaller ones eating the grasses, and thereby benefiting.

In the mountain meadows will be found the California Stipa Grass with plume-like tips, bent in two places. The leaf blades are flat and scattered. The Idaho Bent Grass has shorter branches and a loose spreading flower cluster. The Red Fescue Grass grows up to 3½", the leaf blades feel smooth and soft and are folded inwards. The Bluegrass in the mountain meadows has a narrow flower cluster and grows to 3½" tall. There are many types of bluegrass throughout the Sierra. The Rough-Hair or Tickle Grass with its delicate, slender stems sometimes grow to a foot long. There are various kinds of sedge grasses found throughout the mountains in various soil and moisture conditions.

In alpine meadows the sedge grows in dense tufts with leaf blades narrow and rough. The Pringle's Bluegrass is found here as well as the Timberline Bluegrass with its spikes or purple and stiff stems. The Wood Rush has stiff, erect spikes growing up to sixteen inches.

In the autumn after the first frost these grassland meadows add their own unique beauty to the golden land.

FLOWERS

During the comparitively short growing season from the last snowfall in the late spring to the first snowfall of winter, flowers of many varieties present themselves in breathless haste to complete their life-cycle. There are hundreds of beautiful species growing among rocky ledges, in lush meadows, on sandy slopes, or along streams and in open as well as sheltered areas. Most of the flowers that are prevelent on the east side of the Sierra are found on the west side as well. The most hearty mountaineers that grow among the high altitude rocks are the red and white heather and the sky-blue polemonium. They persevere in such unlikely places as up to 12,000' against the granite skyline ridges.

The MONKEY FLOWER belongs to the Figwort family. Has a brilliant yellow flower with brown spots of about one inch across. The stems are fragile and the leaves very delicate. They like running water and grow in elevations up to 10,000'. Another variety is the spectacular SCARLET MIMULUS
Has a velvet texture and is extremely popular with hummingbirds. The MIMULUS LEWISII, named after Meriweather Lewis, is one of the most beautiful of all. It also enjoys streamsides and is found in a wide range of elevations.

The COLUMBINE, loved by hummingbirds for their nectar in the long flower spurs, belong to the Buttercup family. Blossoms are found to be red, yellow or white. Stems are from 1' to 3' high and slender. They are seen at high elevations to timberline where the blue High Mountain Columbine grows.

The MARSH MARIGOLD belongs to the Buttercup family. The flowers are white with stems erect, from 4" to 12", without leaves. They enjoy moist places at high elevation. Leaves are up to 4" wide.

The LEOPARD LILY or Tiger Lily grow in wet meadows and alongside streams in moderate elevations. Their leaves are whorled and the blossoms are spotted, hence the reference to the spotted animals. They are commonly found in orange-yellow with purple ends in July and August. They like wet banks and are one of the more outstanding varieties of the entire lily family.

LITTLE LEOPARD LILY is found in boggy places in elevations up to 10,000' and are also known for thier sweet, delicate scent.

Another member of the Lily family is the MARIPOSA LILY with their creamy-white petals and dark centers. A cup-shaped flower found in dry, open slopes and flat areas from 6500' to 8000'. The single, erect and stiff stem grow to about a foot in height. Blooms from May to July. Mariposa is the Spanish name for butterfly. Indians liked to eat the roasted bulbs.

The BLUE GENTIAN can be seen in meadows from 7000' to 10,000'. The leaves are short and narrow. Stems can bear a single, erect tubular, terminal flower. Other species such as the tiny white alpine gentian is found in higher elevations while at lower elevations is a gentian with fringed edges to the petals.

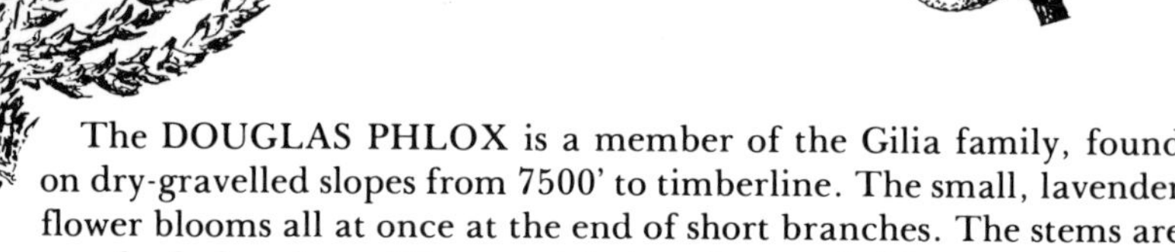

The DOUGLAS PHLOX is a member of the Gilia family, found on dry-gravelled slopes from 7500' to timberline. The small, lavender flower blooms all at once at the end of short branches. The stems are very leafy forming stiff mats with densely crowded leaves.

The SCARLET GILIA is the most spectacular of the Gilia family with its tube-shaped flower. They grow in loose, gravelly soil at moderate elevations. They are sometimes mistaken for the SCARLET PENSTEMON as both flowers are tall with red blossoms. The leaves are divided into long, narrow sections formed at the base of the plant.

The THISTLE POPPY is known for its prickly stems and beautiful white flower with yellow centers. As in all flowers of the poppy family, the petals are very delicate. The stems grow up to 3' and can be seen from 5000' to 8500' along the road.

The COW PARSNIP belongs to the Parsley family. Its white flower with innumerable heads form an umbrella-like cluster, about 6" to 10" wide. The leaves are in groups of three, deeply lobed and toothed from 3" to 12" across. The stems are coarse and hollow. They like damp meadows and streamsides in elevations up to 8000'.

BLEEDING HEART is a member of the Fumitory family. Their rose-purple heart-shaped flowers are clustered near the end of long, naked stems. Leaves with many lobes are from creeping rootstalks. Plants are usually from 10" to 15" high. They are found in shaded wooded areas in high to moderate elevations.

MINERS LETTUCE is a tiny little flower belonging to the Purslane family. The dainty, succulent basal leaves and stems were eaten by Indians and miners as greens. The flower lives in shady spots. The blossoms are a pinky-white with stems growing up to one foot high, bare except for a pair of united leaves just below the flowers.

Another member of the Purslane family is the PUSSY PAWS which grows close to the ground and spreads its dark green leaves out flat. The rose colored flower in a dense cluster is at the end of an erect stem. The stems have few leaves and are about 4" to 10" long. They are found in dry, open areas above 8000'.

The CINQUEFOIL found in high mountain meadows stands 4"-15" high with the short-stemmed basal leaves covered with short, thick, silky hair. The yellow flower has five petals with a mound of pistels in the center. Belongs to the rose family, with numerous species found throughout the mountains.

The CORN LILY grows tall up to 5' high resembling cornstalks. The flowers are dull white, clustered in tassel-like spears. The leaves are large and form dense patches in wet meadows. Indians used this plant for many remedies. It has been mistaken for "skunk cabbage" in the early spring when it first begins to grow.

The SIERRA PRIMROSE grows along granite boulders above timberline, blooming in July soon after the snow melts. The rose-purple blossoms stand on erect stems above basal leaves. It is a tiny plant about 5" high bearing an umbrel of five to ten flowers. Leaves are spoon-shaped and scalloped.
EVENING PRIMROSE is much taller, has a yellow flower, is found along streams and in sandy meadows up to 8000'.

LUPINE belongs to the Pea family. Flowers are blue or pink, crowded together, all whorling around the upper part of the stem. They are common in meadows and various species are found throughout the Sierra. Some grow on dry slopes, other prefer shade, but all are long blooming.

The WHITE and RED HEATHER belong to the Heath family. They grow low in dense mats. The white heather (cassiope—one of John Muir's favorites) has a bell-shaped flower while the blossoms of the red heather is similar to the alpine laurel, also a member of the Heath family. The stem of the red heather has tiny, dark green leaves like pine needles.

The INDIAN PAINT BRUSH is another member of the Figwort family. Flowers are red, 1 to 1½" long, clustered in dense terminal spikes. They are quite common and found in moist meadows up to 10,000'. Closely related to the OWL'S CLOVER

This pink-purplish flower grows in lower elevations, stands erect from 6" to 12" high. The leaves are parted into many narrow segments.

The WILD GERANIUM has pink to white blossoms with petals of deep red veins. The stems stand erect up to 2' high. The leaves are from 2" to 4" wide, rounded and divided into five to seven segments. The plant is very popular, commonly found in meadows or along shaded streams from up to 9000'.

The CALIFORNIA INDIAN PINK, a Pink family member also called Catchfly or Campion. The name "pink" refers not only to the color but to the pinking of the petals. Found in brush or open wooded areas in moderate elevations. The brilliant tiny scarlet blossoms with deep cleft petals are seen from spring to fall. Leaves are from 1" to 3" long, stems about a foot high.

SNEEZEWEED is a member of the Sunflower family. They are very common in meadows and along streams at moderate elevations. The yellow rays droop from the yellow disks with stems branching from 2" to 4" high. The green leaves are about 4" to 10" long.

JEFFREY SHOOTING STAR is a member of the Primrose family. The rose-pink or lavender blossoms are long with a yellow base and distinct purple bank, resembling a cyclamen. Stems are naked, and grows up to 18" high bearing a cluster of five to ten flowers. The leaves are yellowish-green and long shooting up from the base of the plant. They grow in wet meadows or other moist places up to 10,000'

The Wild SWAMP ONION is a member of the Lily family. They are very common, found in wet meadows from 5000' to 9000'. The plant has strong onion or garlic odor as signified by its Latin name Allium. The bulbs are used by mountaineers for food and flavoring. The rose-purple flower is in umbrella-like heads with stout, leafless stems about 2' to 3' high. The leaves are long and grass-like.

FERNS

Graceful gray or green ferns are found under the sequoias and pines of the forest, along cool, moist canyons, or in the shaded, foothill country. Ferns produce spores, not flowers and seed or cones as conifers, but their roots absorb water and minerals from the soil. Some roots have to grow deep to gain the necessary moisture in dryer canyons.

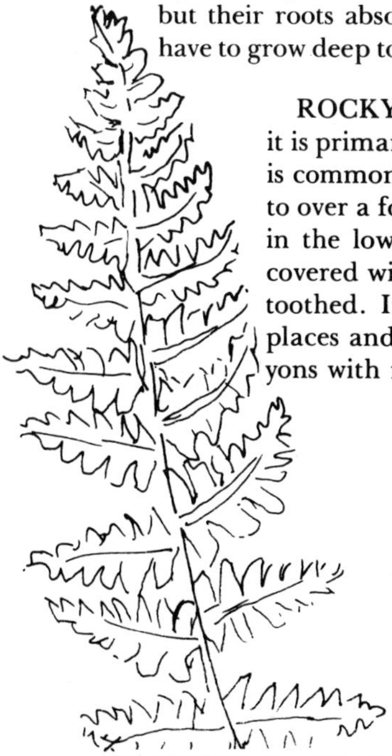

ROCKY MOUNTAIN WOODSIA (Woodsia scopulina): Although it is primarily found in the Rocky Mountains, as the name suggests, it is common in other areas as well. The fronds are numerous from 3" to over a foot long having stripes from 1" to 6" long. Scales are found in the lower part of the dark brown stalk. Fronds are dark green covered with some multi-cellular hairs with segments deeply cut and toothed. It is quite similar to the Fragile Fern and grows in moist places and streamsides from 4000' to 9000'. Also found in cool canyons with moist soil.

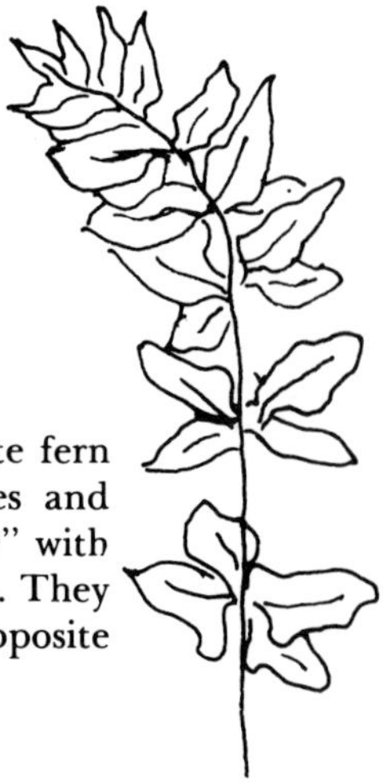

BREWERS CLIFF BRAKE (Pellaea breweri): This delicate fern enjoys high elevations growing prostrate under rocky ledges and straight up when in open meadows. The plants grow up to 9" with fronds in clumps. It is also referred to as the Sierra Cliff Brake. They have two or three leaflets growing together on the main stalk opposite each other.

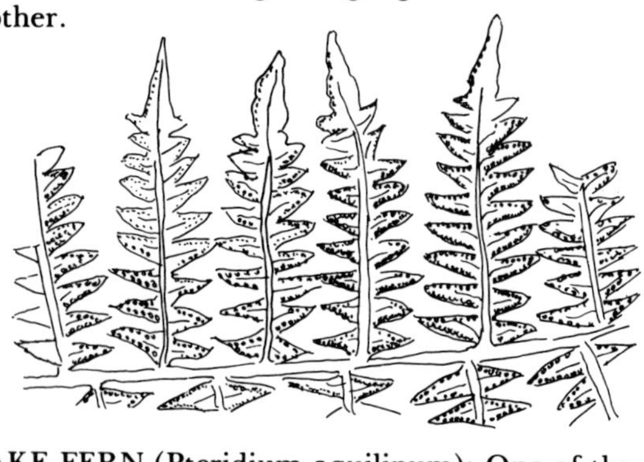

BRAKE FERN (Pteridium aquilinum): One of the most common ferns found in wooded areas or open meadows. It is a coarse, acid-loving fern. They become a dense stand when growing in moist meadows. A single frond is from 2' to 4' high and grows each year from the end of the branch of the long black stem. The underground stem was used for making baskets and textiles by the California Indians. The young tender fronds were eaten by the Indians both raw and cooked.

FIVE FINGER FERN (Adiantum pedatum): Also referred to as the American Maiden Hair not to be confused with the Common Maiden Hair. This plant has slender rootstocks, long fronds forked at the tip of the stripe on strong branches. The stripes are polished, purplish, about 1' to 2' high. The blades are rounded in outline being 8" to 18" wide. It is a common fern found from 3000' to 10,000'. A very distinguished plant, graceful and delicate with the leaf stalks black or brown and sometimes shiny. They grow in moist places protected from the direct sun.

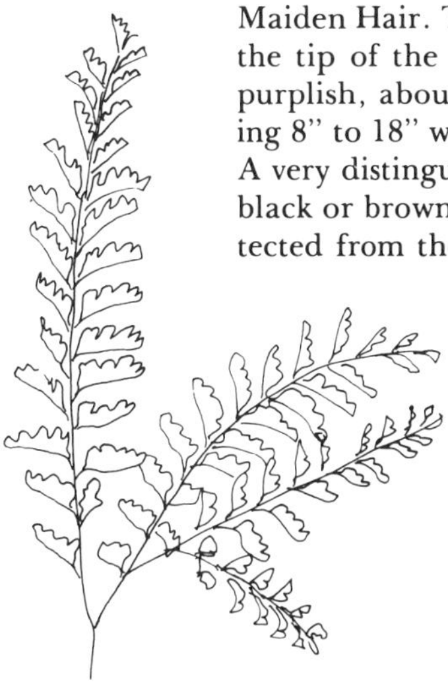

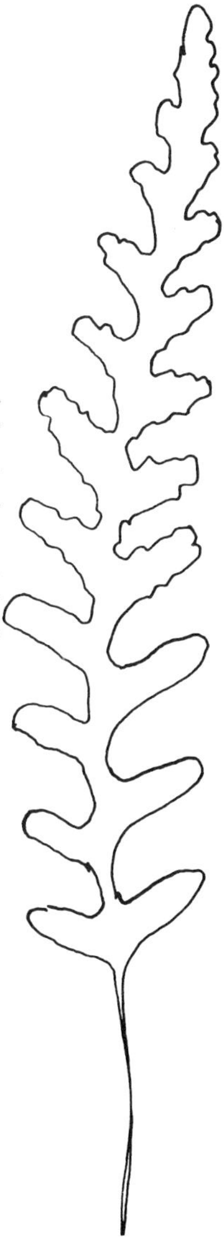

The largest of our native ferns is the GIANT CHAIN FERN (Woodwardia fimbriata). Fronds are up to 8' high with the lobes 4" to 18" long, sori is oblong in cavities in a chain on each side of the midvein. It is reported that the Indians dyed the fibers red with alder bark and used them for their basket and textile designs.

The GOLDEN POLYPODY (Polypodium vulgare) grows in seepage in the shade of granite ledges so the direct sunlight never reaches it. Plants grow to 14" high with pendant fronds, somewhat leathery, and wide spacing, with the sori golden colored when young, hence the name.

PARSLEY FERN (Cryptogramma crispa): American Rock Fern is another name for this plant found at elevations 5000' to 10,000' in cracks of granite. They have two different fronds: the sterile frond is 2" to 8" long with blades 1" to 5" wide. The small sterile fronds are clustered and the branches have a narrow wing with flat leaflets down the stalk. The fertile fronds are taller with no wings on the stalk.

1. ALPINE LADY FERN (Athyrium alpestre) plants are usually large, growing up to 2½' high with very small, round sori in the veins below the center of the frond. Found in moist meadows and along the creeks up to 11,000' elevation. Resembles the Lady Fern found in lower elevations.

2. CALIFORNIA MAIDEN HAIR (Adiantum jordanii) has erect fronds, up to 2' high, distinctive branches along the leaf stalk, fan-shaped pinnules with sori located at the ends of veinlets. Found in the Sierra foothills up to 3000' elevation.

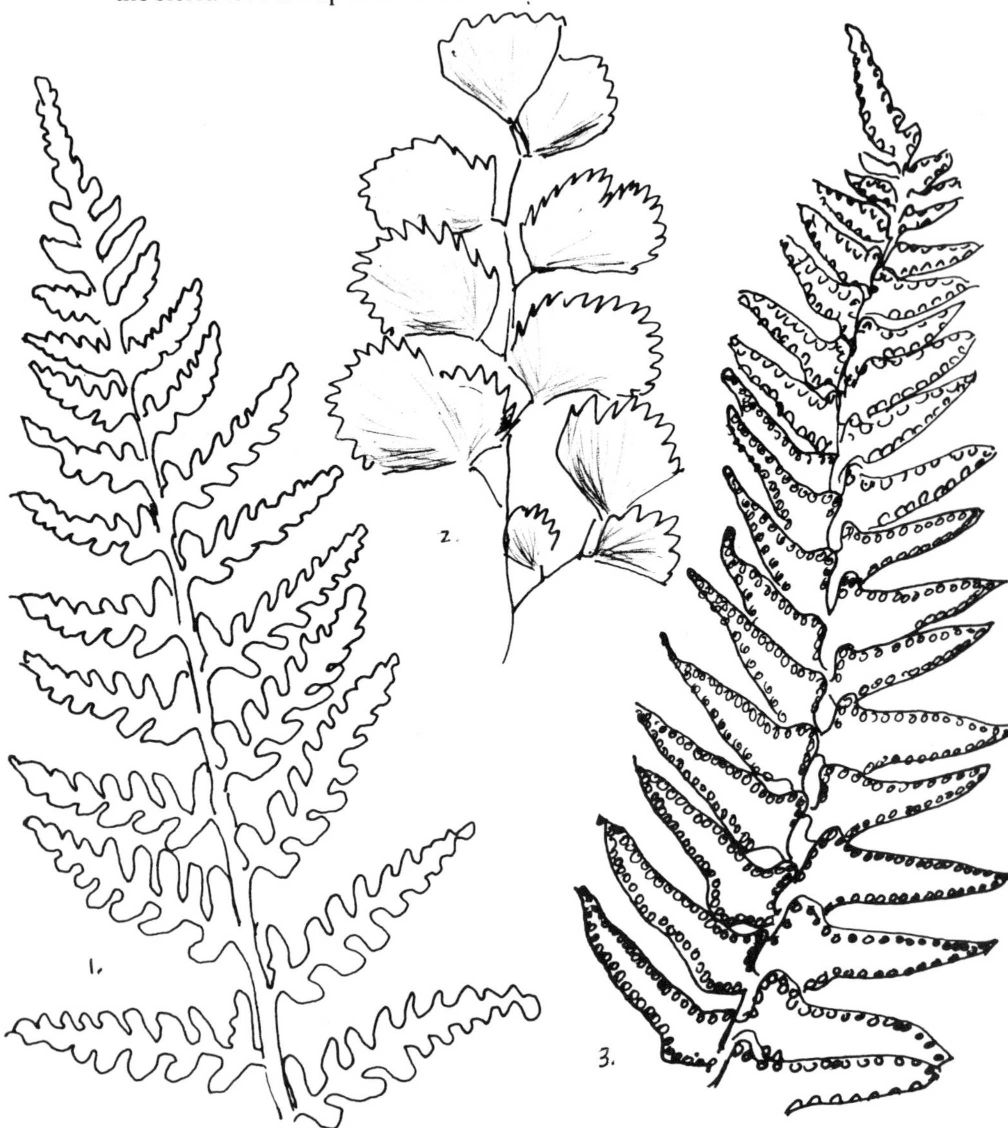

3. SWORD FERN (Polyatichum munitum) is a shiny, evergreen fern that grows up to 3' with stalks, covered with needle-shaped, brown scales. The fronds have an ear-lobe bump at their base. Grows in open areas on the mountain slopes up to 7000' elevation.

ANIMALS

The forested slopes and lush meadows of the Sierra provide a great variety of shelter and food for many kinds of animals, large and small. Here the land, its coverage of trees, shrubs, and grass, plus the moderate summer climate make up an ideal home for them.

Most birds, as well as some of the larger animals such as deer, move down into the foothills below snowline where the winter is less severe. The bear and the marmot prefer to sleep in sheltered caves through the long winter. They store up fat to last them through the hibernation period lasting usually from the middle of December to the middle of April. The chickaree and the cony build special nests in sheltered places and store up enough food to last throughout the winter.

The DEER and the SIERRA NEVADA BLACK BEAR are the two largest and most common animals. Deer depend largely upon leaves of certain brush and trees for food. Each spring they migrate back up the canyons—the buck with short, if any antlers, the does, heavy with fawns, on their way to their summer mountain home. The young black bear are born in the late winter while the mother is in hibernation. Sometimes they are several weeks old when the mother rouses from her sleep. She usually produces offsprings in pairs every other year.

It is evident that the POCKET GOPHER has been around from the earth cores or mounds that run under the ground in long coils. These cores result from activity in winter when the gopher makes tunnels in the snow in search for food. They are tillers of the soil moving many tons of dirt and provide openings for water to penetrate the surface crust down to the tree roots.

CALIFORNIA GRAY FOX lives in the foothills, is the size of a small dog, weighing about 6 to 10 pounds. Has steel gray fur with dark strip down back and tail, white belly, and reddish brown ears.

The YELLOW-HAIRED PORCUPINE is seldom seen but often noted for the girdle marks found on young fir trees. When the boughs or bark are chewed off at the top, it is usually the work of a porcupine. The height above ground is a fair clue as to the depth of the snow when it happened. Known for his quill-covered body, they are unaggressive and good-natured creatures. They shuffle clumsily and can swim as well as climb trees.

The RACCOON has a gray-brown body with hair tipped in black, full tail about a foot long, with alternate black and white rings. Tracks are humanlike in appearance and sometimes is confused with the Ring-tailed cat but is bulkier and darker in color. Usually forages along streams and lakefronts up to 5000' elevation.

The CALIFORNIA RING-TAILED CAT is a very slender animal with a tail the same length as his brown body. Distinctive full tail marked alternately with white and black rings. Seen in Giant Forest and foothill areas. Hunts mice and rats, eats wild fruit and is especially shy.

The BELDING GROUND SQUIRREL, or "picket-pin" is found in the mountain meadows. Its nickname refers to his picket-like stature when on watch near the opening of his burrow. They sit straight up, so straight and stiff by their mounds, then scurry inside when they see danger. They are yellowish brown on the upper sides and a shade lighter underneath. They eat grass, herbs, seeds and hibernate most of the winter—from November to mid March.

The ever-busy CHIPMUNK are found around trees and brush. They are very small, have stripes extending along the sides of their bodies on up across their necks to include the sides of their face. They have a very sharp pointed nose. The GOLDEN-MANTLE GROUND SQUIRREL looks much like an oversized, well-fed chipmunk for which he is often mistaken. His personality is as colorful with his yellow-gold or copperish mantle. The black and white stripes on his sides do not extend to the face as on chipmunks.

The SIERRA PINE MARTEN, resembling a large weasel, is extremely shy, nocturnal in habit and, therefore, seldom seen. The conies, squirrels and chickarees know him all too well as they are his favorite food. Living in rocky crevices at 7000' to 11,000' in the summer, the pine marten stays in trees during the winter.

The SIERRA CHICKAREE are seen from 7500' to timberline. They are heard wherever there are groves of trees and also referred to as the pine squirrel or the Douglas squirrel. They are about the size of a rat, dark brown with buff undersides.

In the highest meadows and slopes adjacent to the skyline crags is found the SOUTHERN SIERRA MARMOT, the largest of the squirrel family. They are vegetarians feeding in the meadows either to get over the long winter or to fatten up for the one to come. They have brownish-gray backs ticked with white, and are buff or yellowish-brown on the undersides. They like to bask in the sun on top of boulders and can be seen along the trail.

The CONY, or pika, a small, pale gray rodent the size of a small bush rabbit, seldom leaves his rocky home except when venturing a few yards into a meadow to feed or cut grass to store in his hay barn for winter. He lives in his burrow under sheltered rocks, tucked away from severe winter cold.

BIRDS

CLARK'S NUTCRACKER: This is a high country bird usually seen at timberline. Has a noisy cry, quite companionable to people. Pale gray body with dark wings, dark center on tail, outer edge of tail feathers and rest of wings in white. Size and habits similar to the Steller's Jay. They enjoy seeds from the Jeffrey and pinyon pine during the winter which they have stored in the fall. All summer they store whitebark pine seeds and in the early spring have food until the new crop of cones are ripe.

The WESTERN EVENING GROSBECK is a camp scavenger of the middle forest region. Has a shrill call; short, black tail with greenish, yellow bill and a black wing with a white patch; stocky body and a black crown.

WHITE-CROWNED SPARROW: Distinguished from other sparrows by black and white stripes on head with one white stripe running above bill through center of crown. Light grayish-brown on back, underparts light. Are seen near thickets in mountain meadows about 7500' to 9000'. Nests on low willow branches, eats insects in summer and seed sprouts in winter. Has a melodious, plaintive song.

WESTERN TANAGER: Their flight in and out of sunlight and shadow is a thing of startling beauty. Vivid scarlet head, upper back and tail dark, wings black with yellow bars, rest of body a striking yellow. Females are drab-green above and yellowish underparts. Their movements are slow and deliberate, building nests towards the ends of branches in the forest from 7000' to 9000'.

The WHITE-HEADED WOODPECKER lives in sequoia groves. Has white head with a red bar; black body; and a white patch on wings. About the size of a robin.

STELLER'S JAY: Large, flashy blue color. Noisy, raucous voice and bold, saucy habits. Eats insects, nuts and grain. Lively companion in camp or along the trail. Large feathered crest on head that is dark, extending to a blue-black on shoulders and wings. Light blue-gray on underparts. Larger than a robin.

ROSY FINCH (Sierra Nevada Rosy Finch): Friendly companion of the high mountain climber. Seen in flocks feeding on snow fields or surface of glaciers. Nests in rocky cliffs along wind-swept ridges above timberline. Bright rosy hue on breast, rump, wings and shoulders. About the size of a sparrow. CASSIN'S PURPLE FINCH lives in lower elevations from 8000' tp 9000'. They forage for buds, insects and seeds. Their size similar to sparrow, rose-red on head with the back, neck, wings and tail brown. Rump, throat and breast a pale rose. Females are brown streaked with gray.

JUNCO (Oregon, Thurber's or Sierra Junco): Has quite dark "cape" over head and shoulders; underside is white. Light brown on shoulders and back, center tail feathers black, outer ones white, legs and feet pink with a light-colored bill. Feeds on ground around base of trees, particularly mountain hemlock or white fir.

AMERICAN DIPPER (Water Ouzel): Perches on rocks in midstream and bobs up and down when standing. Dives under water for food and propels himself with wings when submerged. They eat water insects and larvae. Nests are at waterline or behind the spray of waterfalls. Slate-gray, shading to dark on wings and sides of head. Very stubby tail, large strong legs with sharp clawed feet for the slippery rocks. Sings loudly amid the roaring stream enjoying snow and cold and rain as much as a sunny day.

CHICKADEE (Mountain Chickadee or Short-tailed Mountain Chickadee): Has a persistent, identifying call of "chick-a-dee" or plaintive "ee-chee-chee" heard in the high country. Found on the tip-top twig of the tallest tree. Somewhat smaller than a sparrow. Top of head and throat dark, has white line over eye, cheeks and breast are also white.

AUDUBON'S WARBLER has an unusually melodious song heard toward evening. Blue-gray on underparts; yellow area on crown, throat, on sides near front edge of wings, and on rump. Smaller than a sparrow. Found in areas of oaks and conifers.

ROBIN: They return to the mountains in June. The red breast; black head and tail, gray back and yellow bill heralds spring. They eat worms and are found near mountain lakes and in meadows. They also feed on insects and berries.

BLUEBIRD (Mountain Bluebird): Seen in high country meadows, slightly larger than the sparrow. Feeds on insects from the ground and spends considerable time perched on top of rocks singing. Bright blue all over except for a lighter shade on underside. Females are usually a paler color.

CALIFORNIA QUAIL: The majestic, 10" tall bird has a lower underbody and brown back with breast and side of head blue, brown and with white under throat and his plume is curved forward. Found in the warm foothills, common in Ash Mountain.

FISH

RAINBOW (*Salmo gairdnerii*)

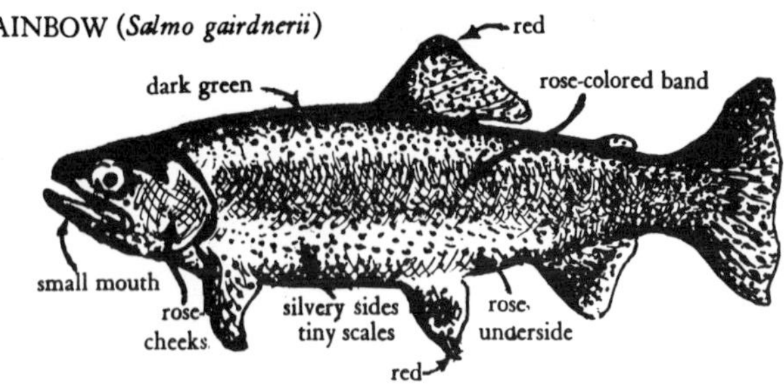

EASTERN BROOK (*Salvelinus fontinalis*)

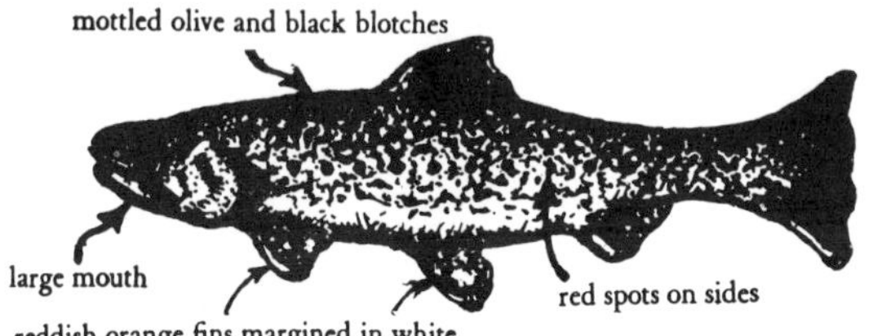

A heavy-bodied, large-mouthed trout. Common above 7,000 ft. Usually frequents deeper holes and slower-moving water than Rainbow. Spawns in the fall.

GOLDEN (*Salmo aqua-bonita*)

dark green

dark spots

scattered dark spots

bright gold on cheeks, underside, and fins

golden-yellow sides

white

bright gold band on sides, and fins

Aqua-bonita means "pretty waters." A native of Kern River country, especially Golden Trout Creek. Spawns in late spring.

BROWN (*Salmo trutta*)
(Sometimes called Loch Leven)

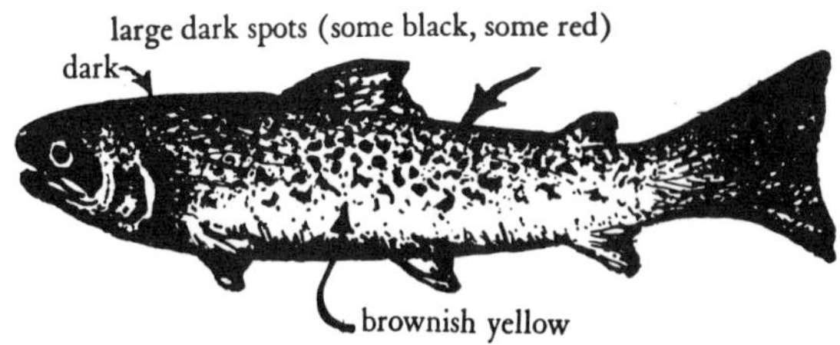

Fishermen, sometimes, have a bad reputation for littering cans, bottles, bait containers and other trash. It only takes a few scattered papers and containers to make a mess. Valuable game fish die because they swallow pop tabs from cans. Children as well as adults cut feet from wading in streams or along the lakeshore from broken glass. Please help save ourselves, the fish we like to catch, our beautiful forests, lakes, and streams by packing out all the litter you pack in.

FRAGILE WILDERNESS

To insure a safekeeping of our fragile wilderness there are a few basic rules that have to be observed. Mountain meadows, alpine tundra slopes and boggy, ungraveled lakeshores have such a short warm season after a long winter, it is up to us who visit their environment to protect them as much as possible. Trampling off the trail, or making another alongside of it in the early season when the ground is wet and spongy, or camping there with or without a campfire can so easily destroy their preciousness we come to see.

From the wilderness point of view, the great predator is man. Even though he helps where he can to reduce his impact on the wilderness, just being there is an adverse impact affecting all creatures. Making camp in a sheltered group of trees near a meadow where water is not too distant pre-empts the nursery room of does with fawn that need such places. Even putting out all fires too well has reduced broad meadows to soured mats and prevented the growth of grassy areas needed by herbiverous animals.

ON THE TRAIL

Taking shortcuts or switchbacks causes erosion plus a great deal of repair work for the trail crew, so keep on the existing trail. Motor vehicles or motorcycles; dogs or any other pets are not allowed on the trails in National Parks. To prevent forest fires, smoke in safe places while stopping and not while travelling along the trail, being positive all the fire is OUT. To protect both the animals as well as yourself, when meeting pack and saddle stock, move off the trail and stay quiet until they pass with no petting.

WHILE CAMPING

Whether for overnight or an extended stay, wood fires for cooking, warmth or aesthetics are allowed only in below 9600' elevations areas. Otherwise chemical fuel stoves are required. Dead or down wood can be burned. The cutting of branches, dead or alive, is prohibited either for fires or in the making of tables, storage caches or bough beds. No new fire rings should be built and, of course, there should be no fires in the fragile meadowland.

The size of the group camping is limited to 25 persons.

Campsites should be 100' from the lakeshore and streams to minimize water pollution and vegetative damages.

Drinking water taken from the streams and lakes should be disinfected by boiling or by chemical treatment as all mountain waters may not be completely safe.

To protect the quality of the water, discharge washing and rinsing water 100' away from the trail, camping area or lake and stream.

It is proper to bury human waste.

There should be no cleaning of fish or soaps deposited in the lakes or streams.

Lastly, observe the old saying: "If you pack it in, pack it out." Trash, bottles, metal foil, unused foodstuffs or pastic wrappers do not nurture an environment.

WILDERNESS PERMITS

The purpose and responsibility of the National Parks are to conserve the scenic or natural beauty or historic objects one comes to visit; to provide protection to the wildlife in their enviornment as much as that which we come to see; and to assist us in the preservation of such for future generations.

Because of the rapid growth of backcountry use in these past few years, quotas have been established by the use of Wilderness Permits to maintain a balance of trail travel, entry over often-used passes and camping in fragile or popular areas. Please check page 78 for complete information on where to write for the areas you wish to visit. Reservations can be made in advance by mail, telephone or in-person. Requests for summer reservations must be submitted between February 1st and May 31st.

INDEX

Fin Dome

WHERE TO WRITE

NATIONAL PARKS

Sequoia–Kings Canyon National Parks
Ash Mountain
Three Rivers, CA 93271

NATIONAL FORESTS

Inyo National Forest
832 N. Main St.
Bishop, CA 93257

Sierra National Forest
Federal Building
1130 "O" Street
Fresno, CA 93721

Hume Lake Ranger District
36273 E. Kings Canyon Road
Dunlap, CA 93621

Cannel Meadow Ranger District
P.O. Box 6
Kernville, CA 93238

Sierra National Forest
P.O. Box 306
Shaver Lake, CA 93664

Sierra National Forest
Trimmer Route
Sanger, CA 93657

IN APPRECIATION . . .

We would like to extend our thanks to those who have given their time and assistance in checking data, maps, and providing special photographs and other interpretive materials making this book as accurate, up-to-date, and useful as possible.

John Palmer, Chief Park Interpreter, of Sequoia, Kings Canyon National Park

Denelle P. Stroh of the Sequoia Natural History Association

Evelyn Batts

The Engineering Department of the Sequoia, Kings Canyon National Park

Nancy Lynn of Sequoia & Kings Canyon Hospitality Service

Personnel of the Inyo National Forest Service

For Special Photographic Credit:

Cover: Eugene Rose

Title Page: Edwin C. (Rocky) Rockwell

Aerial Photograph, Page 9: U.S. Geological Survey

The materials for this guide represents a collection of notes gathered over the past years by Mr. Clark and myself. From a New York City career person in publishing, I first discovered the beauty, awesomeness and grandeur of this vast wilderness on our honeymoon, going down the entire John Muir Trail. While we lived in Sequoia, under the giants when Mr. Clark was a summer Ranger-Naturalist there, we did extensive studying of the Sequoia-Kings Canyon National Parks, and since then, we have explored year after year many other canyons and favorite valleys of this great land.

– Ginny Clark

OTHER GUIDES BY LEW & GINNY CLARK

SEQUOIA-MT. WHITNEY TRAILS $5.95

A companion book to this guide with five-color topographical and four-color area maps, many photographs, trail and nature notes, and descriptive east and north entries which include the Sugarloaf Country and the Cottonwood Lakes-Golden Trout Wilderness. Same size and format; 80 pages, 6" x 9",

YOSEMITE TRAILS $5.95

A complete guide to all the trails in Yosemite National Park with maps—some five color USGS topographic—trail notes, profile charts, showing elevations and mileages between important points. Wildlife notes, forest cover, geology and identification charts of trees and flowers. Many photographs and sketches. Special winter section with ski trails.

MAMMOTH-MONO COUNTRY $4.95

This is The guide to the famous year-round resort area with five-color U.S. topographical and four-color area maps, sketches, many photographs, with lists of services and accommodations. Special winter activities section. 96 pages, 6" x 9".

HIGH MOUNTAINS & DEEP VALLEYS, The Gold Bonanza Days $6.95

The first book of its kind about the Basin and Range Country covering Death Valley, Ghost Towns from Calico to Virginia City, Owens Valley, Ancient Bristlecone Pine Forest and Eastern Approaches to the Sierra with colorful maps, sketches, photographs, wildlife notes, services available, camping notes, and travel conditions.

SIERRA WILDFLOWER PRINT-POSTALS Packet of twelve $2.50

These beautiful, very popular floral photographic prints are in full color. Twelve different favorite Sierra flowers for you to treasure or send to a friend. In plastic packet.